MIRACLES STILL HAPPEN

MIRACLES STILL HAPPEN

Inspiring Real-Life Stories of
Supernatural Intervention

by
Sheri Stone
and
Therese Marszalek

Harrison House
Tulsa, Oklahoma

06 05 04   10 9 8 7 6 5 4 3 2

Miracles Still Happen–
Inspiring Real-Life Stories of Supernatural Intervention
ISBN 1-57794-573-5
Copyright © 2003 by Sheri L. Stone
P.O. Box 1754
Post Falls, ID 83877
and Therese M. Marszalek
PMB111
3327 W. Indian Trail Road
Spokane, WA 99208-9153

Published by Harrison House, Inc.
P.O. Box 35035
Tulsa, Oklahoma 74135

CONTENTS

FOREWORD

$\mathcal{T}$he book you are about to read focuses on miracles, not in an attempt to titillate or to pander to the reader of pulp fiction, but to do exactly what miracles are intended to do. The Latin root for the word *miracle* means a "sign,"[1] and miracles are signs that point to God's Presence in our lives.

Miracles Still Happen is full of signs of God's Presence in the lives of ordinary people. As Christians, we are called to encourage one another because the days in which we live are short. There is nothing more encouraging in the midst of the trials and tribulations of life than to witness God's hand at work in your own life and to know that He has also moved in other situations that are similar to the circumstances, trials, and tribulations that you are now confronting.

This book records many different types of miracles, from people about to be raped and robbed who were miraculously delivered to incredible healings. However, the purpose of these stories is not for us to be entertained or to become captivated by the events themselves, but to find out how God works in the lives of others so that we can know Him better and thereby make Him known to others.

The materialists of our age deny the Presence of God and believe that He is no longer working in the lives of people. The nominalists, and all of those religions with a nominalistic worldview, see themselves as gods and believe that miracles are manifested by merely doing the right thing, holding your breath long enough, or by pronouncing a certain shibboleth.

The stories in *Miracles Still Happen* show that both have missed the point. This book is an incredible alien invasion of our time and space continuum. God continues to reach out of eternity and into quotidian existence to help people face their problems. He wants us to know that He is here, and He wants to have a relationship with us.

God performed the ultimate miracle when He was born as a baby in Bethlehem and when He took away our sins on the cross and was raised from the dead. He has never left us or abandoned us. He said that He would be with us always, and this book proves that His Word is true.

Dr. Ted Baehr, Chairman
Christian Film and Television Commission

The Christian Film and Television Commission is a nonprofit organization committed to educating the entertainment industry and the general public of the media's impact on its audiences. Dr. Baehr also serves as the publisher of "MOVIEGUIDE®: A Family Guide to Movies and Entertainment" and is the author of "The Media-Wise Family."

INTRODUCTION

by Sheri Stone

$\mathcal{D}$uring the 1960s a number of people throughout the world declared that God was dead—and why not? Generally speaking, the church had somehow fallen into silent complacency.

Over the next several years, the popularity of, and involvement in, the New Age Movement and the occult grew so rapidly that they appeared to almost suppress the church's opportunity to demonstrate God's power. While movies, books, TV, Sci-fi, and eastern metaphysical religions demonstrated false supernatural powers, it seemed as if the church did little to challenge the deceptions. However, God continued to pour out His love upon those who chose to believe that He is alive.

In the 1970s an outpouring of the Holy Spirit began to permeate thousands of believers in accordance to biblical prophecy: "And it shall come to pass afterward, that I will pour out my spirit upon all flesh; and your sons and your daughters shall prophesy, your old men shall dream dreams, your young men shall see visions...And I will shew wonders in the heavens and the earth...And it shall come to pass, that whosoever shall call on the name of the Lord shall be delivered..." (Joel 2:28,30,32 KJV). Scores of those who believed witnessed miracles and wonderful displays of God's power, and the events were pondered by many.

In the early 1980s, I was not only crying out to God for a demonstration of His power within the world but also for some mention in the secular media of His greatness within the realm of the church. Eventually, I felt in my spirit that the time was coming when that would happen.

Toward the end of 2000, I again appealed to the Lord about the absence of secular media coverage. He was using Christians around the globe to perform signs and wonders. However, the media hardly paid attention to any of these miracles but intensely bombarded the world with negative subject matter.

As I sought the Lord about this, He led me to put a book together on miracles to share with the world.

It is my hope that this compilation of supernatural miracles from Christians worldwide will help to prove that there is a God and that He is clothed in full regalia. I believe that God wants to demonstrate His power to those who do not believe in Him so they may know Him as their Lord and Savior. He also wants to demonstrate His power to those who know Him as Lord and Savior but do not recognize Him as today's Miracle Worker. To God be the glory!

INTRODUCTION
by Therese Marszalek

*M*iracles. The word itself ignites my spirit.

God has been a Miracle Worker since the beginning of time. From the day He spoke "...Let there be light..." (Gen. 1:3 KJV) and light came into being, He continues to demonstrate His miraculous power throughout the earth. As His explosive might increases in the last days,[1] the word is quickly getting out. God is still in the miracle business!

Since becoming a believer in 1979, I have heard countless people testify about miracles. Hearing these incredible stories of God supernaturally transforming the most hopeless of situations, I wondered, *Why isn't this miracle on the news or being reported in newspapers? People need to hear about the incredible things that God is doing in the earth.*

The secular news media increasingly reports the manifestation of Satan's work through immorality, murder, drug and alcohol abuse, and the gross deterioration of the family. What depressing reports! Why isn't God getting equal billing? It's time for Him to get some press!

Miracles Still Happen is one of many avenues that God is using as a platform to declare His miraculous power. It has been, and continues to be, a tremendous privilege to be actively involved in collecting miracle testimonies from across the globe. All of the testimonies I have heard and read leave me saying, "Wow, God. You are so awesome!"

The following pages contain the stories of people who have experienced supernatural miracles firsthand. For instance, you will meet a woman named Linda who was diagnosed with the HIV virus. With no hope for the future, discouragement weighed her down. However, after God intervened and supernaturally healed her, she was given a new lease on life. Set free from the often-fatal virus, Linda enjoys perfect health today.

You will also meet Al who in 1997 was told that he had ten days to live. However, the God of miracles stepped into the midst of his trial and healed him in such a supernatural way that doctors could only shake their heads.

Is God still performing miracles today? I am fully persuaded that He is, and I suspect that He is just getting warmed up.

Through the many personal interviews I have conducted for this book, I found it interesting that although some people received a miracle after seeking God, others were recipients purely through God's grace. After hearing the stories of those who received His miraculous intervention without seeking it, I asked, "Why, God? Why did You do this for them?"

He answered by reminding me of the many times my thoughtful husband showered me with a beautiful bouquet of flowers when there was no special occasion. I would ask him, "Honey, why did you buy me flowers?"

"Just because I love you," he'd answer with a grin.

God also touches people's lives and showers them with unexpected miracles just because He loves them. The testimonies throughout *Miracles Still Happen* are laced with God's unfailing and endless love. Love, the very core of God Himself, is the common thread that ties these stories together.

It is my desire that the following testimonies will warm your heart and rejuvenate your faith in knowing that God is alive today and loves you beyond human understanding. My deepest desire is for you to experience the greatest miracle of all in personally knowing the God of miracles through a relationship with His Son Jesus Christ.

May God bless you as you catch a glimpse of what He is doing in the earth today.

1

CATAMARAN TO A MIRACLE
by Donna Crowley Meyers

*I*t all happened very quickly. A mere flash in time that came and went like the rumbling of thunder that is here one moment and gone the next.

It was a picture perfect day on Fort Lauderdale Beach. The sun burst from behind puffy, white clouds against a powder blue sky. A gentle breeze whispered through the palm fronds, and the turquoise ocean glistened with allure. Although the tropical winds were not quite what we had hoped they would be, my friend Tony, his buddy from Washington, D.C., and I decided to set sail on Tony's catamaran.

My friend Gina helped us push the boat through the sand and into the water. Because the boat was not large enough to accommodate four people, she opted to stay behind and meet up with us after our voyage.

Tony, his friend, and I quickly waded through the water and jumped onto the catamaran. Tony maneuvered the lines and the sail caught a welcomed gust of wind. Before we knew it, we were gliding across the sea without a worry in the world. *It doesn't get much better than this,* I thought to myself as the ocean spray tickled my face. However, I found that as the day progressed, it would.

Out of nowhere a storm began to rumble. The wind blew, and the rain began to fall. The waves churned with mounting strength as we were swept farther out to sea. As we looked toward the shore, we watched sunbathers run for cover under the canopy of a nearby hotel.

Tony was an avid sailor, so we were not concerned about the storm until we noticed that the boat was not only being pulled out to sea, it was also sinking. "Dear God, please save us," I prayed as we entered the deep, dark water.

The three of us held on to the boat's lines and attempted to swim toward the beach while pulling the boat behind us. Instead of us pulling the boat toward land, the wind pulled us farther away from the shore. We weren't strong enough to fight the force of the storm. We were being pulled out to sea and knew we were going to drown.

Suddenly, a man appeared in the water. "Hold on to the boat. I'll help you," he confidently said as he grabbed the lines and began to swim toward shore.

We were amazed at his strength. He was able to pull the catamaran and us to shore by himself when together, the three of us couldn't budge the boat.

By the time we reached land, the storm had passed and the sun seemed more brilliant than ever. The four of us walked up on the beach together, and I was able to get a better look at our hero.

I had to cup my hand over my eyes to gaze at the stranger standing beside me. He was a tall, slim man, which made it even more amazing that he had the strength to pull us in by himself. The sunlight radiated from behind him, and his face gleamed with a kindness that I had never seen before. There was a peculiarity about him.

"Thank you for saving us," I said with enthusiastic gratitude.

"We couldn't let anything happen to you," he said, smiling.

What an unusual accent. I've never heard one like it, I thought. Just as I was trying to determine his accent, several bystanders ran up to us asking about our unplanned adventure. When I turned back to ask the kind stranger where he was from, he was nowhere in sight. He disappeared as quickly as he had appeared.

"Did you see where that man went?" I quizzed one of the bystanders who watched us come to shore.

"What man?" he asked.

"The man who pulled the boat in for us."

"There were only three people on the beach," he answered. "You and your two friends."

It was a mere flash in time that came and went, one that would change my heart forever.

> *Are not all angels ministering spirits sent to serve those who will inherit salvation?*
>
> HEBREWS 1:14

Donna Crowley Myers is a freelance writer who lives in Pompano Beach, Florida, with her husband, Steven. A playwright and lyricist, Donna's background includes theatre, television, radio, and print. Regardless of the venue, her favorite topic is writing about God and how He moves in the lives of people.

2

THE MIRACLE HERD
by Lavitta Papan

The winter of 1978 had been hard for Don and Lanoma Hendrickson, owners of the Crooked Creek Ranch. First, Don had been in an accident that necessitated back surgery. After his stay in the hospital, he returned to his home on the Snake River in Washington where Lanoma, a licensed practical nurse, cared for him. Because he was laid up for several weeks, he could not tend to his growing herd of calves and depended on his son-in-law, Bob Cooper, to carry the full load of the ranch. Both his wife and daughter helped out as much as possible.

This difficult time suddenly became worse. In December some of Don's calves contracted pneumonia, and by January all 185 were sick. This was serious. If a calf misses two feedings for any reason, it takes two weeks for the animal to regain the lost weight. One hundred eighty-five sick calves could mean disaster.

After six calves died, the vet diagnosed the herd with pneumonia. His only recourse was to treat all of the animals with medication. One calf was in particularly bad shape. The infection spread to its brain, and the medication the vet administered failed to bring relief. It soon died. Working night and day to save the rest of the herd, Bob and his wife never found time to remove this calf's carcass from the barn.

Several days later, twenty-eight seriously ill calves that were wheezing, coughing, and bleeding profusely from their noses were penned in a separate barn. Everyone felt that there was little hope for survival for these calves. The Coopers corralled the remainder of the herd in a feedlot next to the house. These calves had also begun to cough and wheeze. The situation was grim.

God arrived on the scene when Pastor Bill Papen from the Aston, Washington, Full Gospel Assembly of God church, where the Hendricksons and Coopers were members, arrived with his wife and two church members. While the women watched from outside the fence, the three men walked through the feedlots praying over the entire area, claiming victory for their friends.

Don prayed as he viewed the scene from his bedroom window. He then witnessed the sick calves jump up, throw their tails over their backs, and race toward the feeders. What a miracle! From that day forward, none of these calves showed any more signs of pneumonia!

The miracle did not stop there. The men then prayed for the twenty-eight critically ill calves inside the barn. The next morning the calves were no longer bleeding from their noses and neither could a cough or wheeze be heard among them. The once-sick calves were turned into the feedlot with the other healthy calves. The Hendricksons never lost another calf!

A couple of days later Bob was working in the barn and accidentally kicked the little calf that had died the week before. Suddenly, it moved! He immediately began to give it food and water through a stomach tube. Within a few days this "raised-from-the-dead" calf was standing and eating from a manger. This calf had gone fourteen feedings over a seven-day period without food or water.

No wonder Don and Bob called that herd their "miracle calves"!

The apostle Paul refers to the Old Testament provision, "For it is written in the law of Moses, thou shalt not muzzle the mouth of the ox that treadeth out the corn," and asks, "Doth God take care for oxen?" (1 Cor. 9:9 KJV). Yes, He does, and He evidently cares for calves, too![1]

The fruit of your womb will be blessed, and the crops of your land and the young of your livestock—the calves of your herds and the lambs of your flocks.

DEUTERONOMY 28:4

Lavitta Papan and her husband, Bill, have pastored several Assemblies of God churches in the states of Washington and Idaho. Lavitta's beloved husband passed away in February 2000. Since that time she has remained active in women's ministries, nursing homes, and Christian television broadcasting.

3

EVEN THE WIND AND RAIN OBEY HIM
by Dr. Flo Ellers

*E*arly one morning in 1985 I received a phone call from Sister Henysel, a missionary who visited our village of Klawock, Alaska, asking me if I would preach at an outdoor crusade in Mexico. Still groggy and not realizing what was being asked of me, I quickly agreed to her request.

"Wonderful!" she said. "I'll call the pastors and encourage them to start fasting and praying for the crusade." Thirty-one pastors in Mexico supported this effort.

I hung up the phone and suddenly had butterflies in my stomach. "Lord," I said in a panic, "What have I done? I've never held a crusade in my life!" A wave of peace flooded over me, and I intuitively knew that everything would be fine.

Sister Henysel had received my newsletter for a number of years and had read about the people who had received salvation and whom God had touched in the many places I had ministered. The one thing I didn't mention in the newsletter was that I only shared my testimony of salvation in the meetings; I never preached.

I have received invitations from across the globe to give my testimony, share in song, and give an altar call. Apparently Sister Henysel and the Mexican pastors thought I must be a "great" international evangelist because I travel worldwide.

One month before the Mexican crusade, I sang at a crusade in Uganda. When the crusade ended, our leader, Brother Victor Onuigbo, prayed for me so I would receive the ability to preach.

After leaving Uganda I flew to Mexico to begin the crusade, never having preached before in my life. Thousands of people were waiting to hear about God, His signs and miracles. God did not disappoint. Shortly after I walked onto the outdoor platform, His power took over and many miracles occurred.

As I preached a storm began to brew. Black boiling clouds covered the sun and huge gusts of wind carried away everything that wasn't tied down, including my notes. Soon a torrential rain began to beat on the sound equipment and on the microphone in my hand. The crew and I were in danger of being electrocuted. People began to run from the crusade seeking protection and covering.

I must ignore this torrential storm, I thought. Looking down at my Bible I planned to read the Scriptures I had prepared. Suddenly I became very angry at the wind and rain. *How dare you keep the people from hearing God's Word,* I screamed to myself.

I opened my mouth and in an authoritative, booming voice roared: "In the name of Jesus, I take authority over this wind and rain, and I command you to stop *now* in Jesus' name!"

The wind immediately stood still, and the rain instantly stopped. In shock, my mouth fell open. Thousands of people who witnessed the phenomenon stared at the sky in awe. Praise began to ripple across the audience.

I continued on with my sermon; after I had finished preaching, someone tapped my shoulder and said, "There's a man in the balcony who is lame and can't walk. He wants you to come and pray for him."

"*We'll* go and pray for him," I replied, and I asked several ministers to join me. I didn't want anyone to look at me as if *I* was the one healing him.

Approaching the lame man, we felt a whirlwind of God's power swirling around him. In accordance with Scripture, the ministers and I laid our hands on him. Startled by the power of God, he stood up straight. He could hardly believe that he was standing. He took a few stiff steps before he began to walk. The congregation shouted, "Gloria Dios! Gloria Dios!"

When the altar call was given, nearly 500 people rose from their seats to accept Jesus Christ as their Lord and Savior!

The men were amazed and asked, "What kind of man is this? Even the winds and waves obey him!"

MATTHEW 8:27

After graduating from Bible college in 1982, Flo Ellers completed her doctorate in 2000. Through her itinerate ministry, Global Glory Ministries, she preaches the Gospel to the nations with signs, wonders, and miracles following.

4

THE GIFT

by D. F. Higbee

$\mathcal{O}$ne frigid January morning, the streets of Spokane, Washington, were covered with thick layers of ice and snow. After starting the pickup, the old truck was almost too cold to move; but putting the vehicle in drive, my mother and I crept to the intersection. Thinking I had time to cross four lanes of traffic, I stepped on the gas. The truck lurched forward into the oncoming lanes and died. The cars couldn't stop, and the truck wouldn't re-start after it had stalled. Mom and I braced for the impact. I prayed with my eyes closed. I thought that dying with my eyes shut wouldn't hurt as much.

The cars smashed into the driver's side of the pickup, some hitting the truck directly over the gas tank. The impact spun us around 360 degrees. When I opened my eyes, I wondered why we were still alive and not scattered across the street in bloody, broken pieces. Miraculously, the pickup still worked, although somewhat scrunched. After exchanging insurance information with the other drivers, we drove home.

I took the truck to the body shop and sat in the waiting room while the men stripped the rear quarter panel from the vehicle. After hearing the men whisper among themselves, one of them approached me with the panel in his hands. "This i-i-isn't possible," he stammered. "It c-c-couldn't have happened that way. You should be dead."

When I asked him to explain, he showed me the quarter panel. The scrunched metal clearly showed the impact of the cars on the outside of the panel. However, on the section of the panel that covered the truck's gas tank, the indentation came from the *inside* of the panel.

The repairman said, "It's as if a force from the inside pushed against the panel to keep the gas tank from exploding when the oncoming cars hit your truck. Not possible," he said.

He didn't know about the gift.

The gift began in 1952 with a 39-year-old woman named Emma. Emma had lost eight full-term babies because of an Rh incompatibility. And in late October, she became keenly aware that she was pregnant once again.

Emma nervously twisted her purse straps as she balanced on the edge of the waiting room couch. Time seemed to stand still. When Dr. Jane Gumprecht called her back to the examination room, she carefully scrutinized Emma's face, searching for signs of emotional breakdown. As the doctor leaned over with her stethoscope to listen for a heartbeat, Emma reassured her that the baby was alive.

Dr. Jane gently squeezed Emma's shoulder. She hadn't heard a strong heartbeat, and the baby hadn't moved. She was worried. Emma's family had been less than supportive through the previous losses of babies, and this pregnancy appeared hopeless.

"Doc, I just know it will be fine this time. I have to try. I want my husband back!" she cried. "He blames *me* for the deaths of the other babies." Desperation shook her voice as tears spilled down her cheeks. Scrambling off the examination table she headed for the door.

"Emma, we'll try our best. I'll talk to your husband. Maybe I can make him understand that it's not your fault." Dr. Jane bit her lip as Emma bolted out the door.

It was unlikely she could make Emma's husband understand. Medical technology simply had no cure for the Rh hemolytic disease of the newborn that killed nearly 3,500 babies a year in the early 1950s. Blood cells from the fetus found their way into Emma's bloodstream, causing her body to create antigens that attacked and destroyed the red blood cells of the baby. These babies died before ever reaching the birth canal. None of the treatments in place at the time were effective in birthing healthy babies.

Emma slammed through the back door of her home and skidded to a stop on her knees under the kitchen table. She prayed hysterically, "Jesus! Jesus! Please give me a live baby. My husband hates me. Just let this one live. You can *have* the baby, just let it live, please!"

A warm, loving sensation flooded Emma's thoughts. The tears stopped. She stood up knowing beyond a shadow of a doubt that the baby would live. Not everyone had that same faith, as the next several months proved agonizing for her and her family. Her husband's hostility increasingly grew as the nine months wore on.

On the first day of April 1953, Dr. Jane sent Emma to a nearby hospital for a C-section and a blood transfusion for the baby. Babies undergoing this procedure were generally jaundiced and usually brain-damaged, if they lived at all. But she had to try.

On April 2 at 5:53 P.M., Emma gave birth to a 7 pound, 3 ounce baby girl. Severely jaundiced, the child was placed in an incubator after a blood transfusion. Though the next two weeks were critical,

Emma never doubted the outcome. The medical staff, however, didn't share her viewpoint.

The surgeon who performed the procedure came by Emma's room and sat down on the edge of her bed. He pressed a piece of paper into her hand and gently explained that the baby would be seriously brain-damaged. He soberly suggested that she should consider putting her daughter in an institution. Even if the baby survived, he claimed, she would most likely be emotionally uncontrollable due to the mental problems she would face.

With tears welling in her eyes, Emma pushed his hand back and said without flinching, "No! God gave me a live baby, and she will be just fine."

Soon it came time to take the baby home. After a few family squabbles, they finally settled on a name. Emma told her Asian nurse that the child's first name would be "Dorothy" after her grandmother, and "Faye" would be her middle name. Little Dorothy Faye came home to an ecstatic family and a bright new nursery.

Something else came home with the new family, a gift not yet understood. As the child grew and entered school, it became obvious that the little girl had no evidence of the brain damage reported by the medical staff. Her I.Q. tested between 139 and 150, and she graduated from both high school and college with high honors. God's plan didn't concur with the medical diagnosis.

In 1978, Emma discovered the gift. She opened a book of names and learned that *Dorothy* means "God's gift" and *Faye* means "faith." Emma understood—the gift of faith, the gift of a child; but more importantly, the gift of life.

One fleeting moment in the Presence of the Most High God had given Emma the strength to believe God's best for her child. After the gift of life was born, she passed her faith on to the little girl, reminding her often that she was a miracle. And if she was a miracle, then God had a purpose for her life. I have never forgotten. You see, Emma is my mother.

> *For you created my inmost being; you knit me together in my mother's womb.*

PSALM 139:13

Faye Higbee has worked in the support services of law enforcement for over 28 years. She is a drama coach and a praise and worship leader as well as a writer/photographer. Faye is also active in A Company of Women, a national women's ministry. Faye is married and has two stepchildren and one grandchild.

5

ARIZONA ANGEL
by Sara O'Meara

My husband, Bob, and I, along with our good friends, Yvonne and her husband, Don, had just finished helping our daughters settle in at Arizona State University. It was their first year away from home, and we wanted to make sure that everything was okay. Saying our good-byes we got in our van for the trip back to Los Angeles.

As we left Phoenix, we stopped at an all-service gas station to pick up some cold drinks and ice for the trip. After filling the gas tank, Yvonne got behind the wheel as the rest of us climbed into the van, making ourselves comfortable for the long trip home.

We had traveled for quite some time when Bob said, "I thought the sun set in the west!"

I am not good with directions and hadn't noticed that we were traveling the wrong way. Yvonne had turned east when we pulled out of the filling station. We had been on the road for an hour and a half before Bob noticed. We immediately turned around and headed toward Los Angeles.

After traveling for three hours, we again pulled into the gas station that we had stopped at earlier. We looked at one another and laughed. What else could we do?

After filling the tank, we headed home. We had traveled for what seemed like an eternity when all of a sudden, we heard a thump. We were in the middle of nowhere and had a flat tire. *What next!* I thought.

There were no other cars on the road. Every now and then a truck would whip by, sending up swirls of dust and making our van shudder like a piece of paper. With no one to help, we had no choice but to change the tire ourselves. Because the car jack and spare tire were under the floor of the van, we had to remove everything we had packed in the van.

Unfortunately, Yvonne and I had packed our clothes in plastic bags; with every gust of wind, the bags went flying across the desert countryside. We chased after the runaway clothes for fifteen minutes. In the meantime our husbands struggled to fix the flat tire with an inadequate jack. Hot and tired, Yvonne and I returned to the van only to find that Bob and Don had been unable to jack up the van.

"We'll just pray for someone to help us," I said.

"There's no way someone will stop to help us, " Don said.

While everyone stood around the car, I silently prayed for help.

Out of nowhere an old, funny-looking truck came chugging down the road and pulled up behind us. A little one-toothed man appeared from out of the cab of the truck.

Yvonne was so fascinated with his single tooth that she didn't really listen to what he was saying. We told him about our problem and asked if he would call someone to help us after he reached his destination.

He quickly replied, "No need for that. I have a hydraulic jack in the back of my truck."

What a surprise!

The little man sauntered back to his truck and pulled out the jack. We all watched in amazement as the side of the van was lifted with one press of his foot. The tire was replaced in minutes.

The four of us stood there a moment admiring his miraculous handiwork. When we turned around to thank him, he and his truck had both vanished. Checking both directions on the long stretch of open highway, we saw no sign of him anywhere. He couldn't have started his truck and driven away without our noticing. He had miraculously and mysteriously disappeared.

We all looked at each other and in unison said, "That must have been an angel!"[1]

God is our refuge and strength, an ever-present help in trouble.

PSALM 46:1

Sara O'Meara, formerly a Hollywood starlet, cofounded Childhelp USA®, a national nonprofit organization dedicated to meeting the physical, emotional, educational, and spiritual needs of abused and neglected children. Sara is married to Robert Sigholtz, Ph.D. She has a son and two stepdaughters. Another son, Charles, died in an auto accident in 1988.

6

RIDE TO RECOVERY

by Pastor Ivan Roberts

In the summer of 1950, I helped my father do carpentry work. On the morning of August 8, a group of friends invited me to join them on a trip to Canada. It happened to be a day that my father and I were unable to work because we lacked building materials. I happily accepted the invitation.

"They're going to practice for the championship softball game," I lied to my mother, "and they asked me to practice with them." I fabricated a story, suspecting that if I told her the truth, she would forbid me to go.

To avoid arousing any suspicions, I cleverly arranged for my friends to pick me up in a remote spot. While waiting at the corner, I felt uneasy about deceiving my mother. I was even tempted to return home. The anxious feeling hung over me until my friends and I were far out of town.

Driving in Harold Nichols' 1948 Mercury convertible, we headed for Christine Lake in British Columbia. What a day of fun! The sun shone brightly while my five pals and I anticipated a grand old time.

After our fun in the sun, we jumped back in the convertible to head home. "Do you want to drive, Ivan?" Harold asked with a grin.

I quickly took him up on his offer and without hesitation hopped in the driver's seat.

As we rounded a sharp curve just north of Republic, Washington, the car veered off the road, slid onto the shoulder, and hit a deep chuckhole. I lost control of the car and in trying to get it back on the road, the car flipped upside down. Everyone came out of the accident unscathed, except for me. When the car came crashing down upon us, it landed on my head.

One of my friends ran to a nearby farmhouse to call for an ambulance while the others tried to lift the vehicle off of my trapped head. My friends knew I was in grave danger and fervently prayed for God's help. The ambulance arrived in moments and quickly sped me to the nearest hospital.

The hospital director called my parents in Spokane informing them of the seriousness of my accident. After telling them I might not live, my grief-stricken father collapsed.

Because of my father's emotional state, his friend, Vern, volunteered to transport my parents to Republic. Although the doctors offered no hope of recovery for me, Vern and my parents called several prayer groups requesting them to pray for a miracle.

Five days later I was transferred to St. Luke's Hospital, now known as St. Luke's Rehabilitation Institute in Spokane, Washington. While at St. Luke's, I became disruptive and unable to be left alone. My condition worsened as my mind reverted to that of a small child. My increasingly agitated and disruptive behavior forced the hospital staff to relocate me to a medical facility better equipped to handle my unexplained outbursts. They wanted to place me in a psychiatric ward, but my mother refused to let them. She insisted on taking me home.

Because Mother did not believe in taking medication, I was not given anything for pain relief, which I so desperately sought. The sharp, throbbing pain in my head became so unbearable that I attempted suicide.

As the physical pain became more intolerable, my mind began playing tricks on me. I often thought I was some kind of an animal.

The infection in my head raged. My white blood count skyrocketed and my fever dangerously climbed to 107 degrees. Even with such a high fever, I shook with chills.

Unable to handle my deteriorating condition, my parents finally called our doctor. After he arrived, he said, "I have a jacket that will keep you warm, Ivan." Wasting no time, he put me in a straight jacket and committed me to St. Luke's psychiatric ward.

Leather restraints padlocked me to a bed in my small cell in the psyche ward. Because of the brain injuries, I did not have the ability to reason or understand where I was.

"Ivan will never recover," the doctor told my parents. "He'll have to be taken care of for the rest of his life."

My mother refused to accept his grave report. "Do you want a minister to come and pray for you, Ivan?" she asked.

"Yes," I agreed.

When the minister entered my cell, he asked, "Do you believe in God?"

"Yes."

"Can I pray for you?"

"Yes."

"The next time I see you, Ivan, you'll be completely whole." Placing his hands on my forehead, he prayed a short prayer asking God to heal me and then left.

My mind was instantly restored. Jesus visited me and healed me! I testified to everyone who came into my cell. You can imagine that my healing did not go over very well in the psyche ward.

When the ward doctor visited me, I asked him if he believed in Jesus and His ability to heal. I learned that he was not only a medical doctor, but also a Bible college graduate. "I do believe Jesus healed you, Ivan. But I can't release you from the psyche ward until I can medically prove you are healed."

He immediately ordered the hospital staff to run tests. My white blood cell count had dropped abruptly, and by two o'clock that afternoon, I was moved to a private room with a view that overlooked the Spokane River. The raging infection in my brain was gone! Two weeks later I was released from the hospital.

After I returned home, I lost the sight in my right eye. Dr. Lynch, the brain specialist who cared for me at Sacred Heart Hospital, told me it was a miracle that I could see at all. "Medically, it should be impossible for you to see," he said. The damage to my skull was so extensive that bone fragments had destroyed nerves and many parts of my brain.

Two years after the accident, I enlisted in the military and spent four years in the Pacific Theater. To this day I don't know how I was accepted in the military with documented blindness in one eye.

Fifty-two years after the accident, I enjoy perfect health and continue to thank the Lord for praying people and for a God who heals.

"And these signs will accompany those who believe: In my name they will drive out demons...

...they will place their hands on sick people, and they will get well."

MARK 16:17,18

Pastor Ivan Roberts and Ruth, his beautiful wife of thirty-six years, have four children and eight grandsons. After Ivan retired from the postal service, he entered the ministry as a visitation minister and service coordinator. He has also been a chaplain in hospitals and nursing homes for the past sixteen years.

7

THE CREATION OF A NEW WOMB
by Janet Rutherford

*A*fter the premature birth of my daughter, Jamie, in 1979, I was informed that cancer saturated my lungs and uterus. I immediately underwent surgery followed by one year of intense chemotherapy at the University of Washington Medical Center cancer ward.

In 1983 I married Scott and became a mother to his eight children. I scrambled to read everything I could about raising children and teenagers. Although Scott and I were blessed with so many beautiful children, I wanted to have more children of my own.

A few years after the cancer surgery, I began to experience abdominal pain and discomfort. In 1985 Dr. Palo at Swedish Medical Center in Seattle, Washington, performed a laparoscopy to remove a significant amount of scar tissue that had developed in my uterus.

After the lengthy operation, I asked Dr. Palo what my chances were of having more children. He said, "Janet, we would literally have to recreate your uterus for you to have another child. The surgery is expensive and not always successful." He then added the final blow. "This procedure isn't covered under your insurance either. I'm sorry." The doctor's report indicated that I no longer had a womb.

That's when the Lord took over and began to work a miracle in my body.

In 1987 I attended a church pastored by Dave Johnson. He preached a powerful message on God's plan to give us the desires of our hearts. Pastor Dave then invited people to come forward for prayer to receive the things they so desired.

Because I had been so deeply moved by Pastor Dave's message, I felt as though the Lord was speaking directly to me. In nervous anticipation I made my way to the altar.

Pastor Dave asked me, "Sister, what are your heart's desires?"

"I want to have children either by my womb or by adoption," I said.

"Which would you prefer?"

"By my womb," I answered. A calm reassurance washed over me as he prayed a simple prayer of faith.

One year later I gave birth to a beautiful baby boy. We named our child after Pastor Dave and affectionately call him David. The biblical meaning of his name is "beloved."[1]

The night God recreated my uterus He also delivered me from anorexia and bulimia, diseases in which one has a distorted view of her body image. Bulimia leads to overeating, purging, and an abnormal preoccupation with food. Anorexia involves an abnormal fear of being fat and leads to barely eating food at all. After being plagued with this sickness for twelve years, God instantly set me free from this devastating illness. The Lord truly gives us the desires of our heart!

> *Delight yourself in the Lord and he will give you the desires of your heart.*
>
> PSALM 37:4

Janet Rutherford and her husband, Scott, have been married for nineteen years and are the proud parents of eleven children. She is an active Sunday school teacher and worship leader. Janet also shares her musical talents at weddings, funerals, and the famous Enzion Inn in Leavenworth, Washington, the beautiful town where Janet and her family live.

8

CANNING-DAY SPECIAL

by Sheri Stone

"*Jeannie*, would you hold down the fort while I take another count?" I asked before heading to the storage building. "I'll keep an eye on you to make sure you don't get swamped with customers."

"Sure," Jeannie agreed. "I think I'll sit down and rest my aching body before anyone else comes."

The lull in business gave me time to step into the storage building a few feet behind the produce stand. We had featured another one of our canning-day specials, and the sales were so good that our produce had been depleted. I needed to take a quick inventory to restock our supplies.

Soon I heard a car drive up front. Peeking around the door, I saw two men get out of a green van. I turned back to the room thinking, *They must be picking up tomatoes for their wives.*

No sooner had I thought this than the Holy Spirit warned me of impending danger. Dropping to my knees, I uttered a panicked prayer. "What's going on, Lord?" I blurted. "Who are those men? Why are they so dangerous?"

Shaking in fear, I prayed but then stopped for a moment. *Fear...that's strictly Satan's device, and I won't fall to it,* I thought. "Father God, give me the strength to stand against this fear."

I pressed on in prayer. The power of the Holy Spirit surged through me with the force of lightning, causing the fear to flee like a flock of frightened geese.

I peered through a small window and saw that the warning was valid. The two men were giving Jeannie a terrible time.

Both men appeared to be at least six feet tall and around 200 pounds. They shared a combination hippie, lumberjack look that consisted of long, unkempt hair, five-o'clock beards, tattered jeans, worn shirts, and sleeves rolled up to their shoulders. I guessed them to be in their mid-thirties.

One man, hands on hips, scowled. The second was more aggressive and threateningly leaned over the produce counter. Even though Jeannie looked calm I thought, *I'd better get out there fast.*

"Don't go yet!" came an explicit command in my spirit. "Continue to pray until I give you a release."

No time for debate. I prayed, rebuked, and commanded the spirits to dispel. It seemed like forever but actually only took a minute before the release came. The Lord was now in control. Out I went, ready for war!

Jeannie was smiling, even though the men now stood on both sides of her. Surprised by my entrance they momentarily withdrew. I moved to Jeannie's side trying not to give them benefit of my fore-knowledge. Smiling, I questioned, "May I help you, gentlemen?"

"Yeah." The first man immediately drew closer to Jeannie. "We've come to take you pretty ladies for a ride in our van."

"Thank you, but we have to tend to business," I said, appearing unconcerned. To prove their threats meant little to me, I continued, "Besides, we aren't that type of women."

"That doesn't matter to us, honey," the more aggressive man growled. "You're coming anyway!"

We knew this man was serious, but because our hearts were turned to God, we chimed, "No, we're not!" The smiles stayed imprinted on our faces.

The second man moved nearer to me. At any moment he would grab my arm. He hissed louder, "We are taking you ladies with us, and there's nothing you can do about it. Now, get in that van!"

It no doubt frustrated them that they were unable to touch us. It was as if an invisible shield protected us, and the men were physically incapable of fulfilling their threats.

Without any fear Jeannie confidently said, "You still don't understand. We don't have to go with you regardless of what you say or try to do." In a single voice we chorused, "Our God will protect us!"

"Your God!" the aggressive man jeered. "That's stupid. Your God means nothing to us. Don't you know, lady? Can't you tell? We're Satan worshipers, and our god is powerful enough to destroy you. Get into that van before we force you!"

The first man grabbed for Jeannie, and the second stepped toward me. I drew back and in a booming voice said, "Greater is He that is in us than he that is in the world and that means you and your god. In the name of Jesus, get away from us!" I commanded.

At that order both men were paralyzed in their tracks. Almighty God had rendered them powerless. Realizing he witnessed a force unknown to him, the first man sprinted to the van, jumped inside, and slammed the door.

The second man, stunned by the power of the Lord, stood there. Tears welled in his reddened eyes. "W-w-who is your God?"

he stammered. His hands were again on the counter, but now it was because his legs couldn't support the weight of his hobbling body. "Nothing like this has ever happened before. No one has ever been able to stop me. *This* has to be a supernatural power."

"Our God is Jesus Christ, and He is the God of everything. Your god became powerless merely at the mention of His name," I said.

Jeannie continued, "As you just saw, your god has no power over us. You couldn't even get near."

Choking back the tears and exhausted by the experience the man whispered, "For ten years I've been looking for what you have. I've tried everything but nothing has ever satisfied me. Your God is my answer. He *must* be the answer!"

The man who had been aggressive only a few minutes before was now sobbing. "What must I do to know Him?" he asked.

Jeannie and I bounced with excitement. "Sir, all you have to do is ask for forgiveness of your sins, invite Jesus into your life as your Lord, and turn from your old ways," Jeannie said. "That's it. You'll see a spectacular change in everything you do."

I agreed. "You won't believe the changes God will bring about in your heart."

The man repented from his sins and received Jesus into his life. He was transformed before us. Tears flowed and his face shone as he thanked us again and again. We were thrilled and shared in his celebration but were caught off guard when he suddenly announced, "You have customers. I'll go." He stepped back.

"You needn't leave," Jeannie pleaded.

"I-I-I have to go now. Good-bye and thank you." Before we could say anything more, he hopped into the green van and was gone.

Jeannie and I were dumbfounded. In less than fifteen minutes, a man had stepped into our lives, threatened us, received Christ into his heart, and stepped back into the world. We didn't even know his name.

"What glory Your power provides, Lord. Keep him safely in Your care," we prayed. Then brushing back tears, we again began to serve our customers.

The following year my booming produce business outgrew the stand and was transplanted into a larger building. Jeannie moved away, and I hired Leta to take her place.

Canning season brought crates of vibrantly colored fruits and vegetables. The store overflowed with people, making it difficult to offer personal service to everyone. Leta helped with the outside customers, and I stayed inside and ran the cash register.

Twice I peered around the mass of customers to ask the handsome, well-dressed gentleman near the ice cream counter if I could help him. Both times, he shook his head saying, "No, I'm just waiting." A little boy holding the man's hand smiled.

"They sure are patient," I commented to a customer.

I continued helping my customers. A half-hour later the crowd thinned. I was exhausted but took advantage of the lull to go outside to help Leta replenish the produce.

I had only taken a few steps when I realized the man and the little boy still stood by the ice cream counter. "Oh, sir," I apologized, "I thought you were waiting for someone. I didn't realize you were still here. Can I help you?"

A smile crossed his now glowing face. Tipping his head toward me he replied, "You already have, ma'am. You already have." With the child by his side, he walked past me, out the door, and around the corner of the building.

Watching through the side window, I tried to place his face. I didn't remember who he was until he turned, waved, and stepped into his green van.

> *I have given you authority to trample on snakes and scorpions and to overcome all the power of the enemy; nothing will harm you.*

LUKE 10:19

Sheri Stone is the director of The International Network of Christians in the Arts and the Songbird Christian Performing and Fine Arts Center, headquartered in Coeur d'Alene, Idaho. She is coauthor of this anthology as well as a screenwriter with her husband, Gene. The Stones have been married over forty years.

9

GRANDMA LIVES!

by Gena Bradford

"*G*ena, your grandmother is in a hospital in Louisville. She has suffered a cerebral hemorrhage and is in a coma." I felt as though a boulder had crushed me. Could this really be happening?

I received my mother's phone call a week before I was scheduled to go on my first trip back home since my childhood. I intended to visit my grandmother, whom I had not seen since I was twelve. Now that I had four children of my own, I longed to know my grandmother and learn of my heritage.

Time with my grandmother had always been rare. Being raised in a military family, we moved frequently when I was a child. After my father retired, we never moved back to Kentucky; and money was seldom available for vacations. Eventually, I married and settled in Spokane, Washington.

I never stopped thinking about the family I hardly knew. I had longed to get to know my aunts, uncles, cousins, and Grandma Carrie. I planned this trip for six months and could hardly wait to go. Our finances barely covered our monthly living expenses, so I borrowed the money for the plane ticket. Grandma was eighty-four years old. During my prayer time, I sensed an urgency to see her. Now I understood why. She was dying, and I was fearful that I had waited too long.

I often imagined the conversations I longed to have with her. *What was your life like on the farm raising your six children? What was my grandfather like? Did you keep a diary or a journal, and will you share it with me?* And most importantly, *Grandma, do you love the Lord Jesus?* How could I ever forgive myself if Grandma died before I knew these precious answers? Grief filled my heart as the news of her condition shattered my reunion fantasies.

That night I prayed, "Lord, I can't bear the loss of not knowing Grandma Carrie. She's a part of me. My heritage comes from her. I want to touch her, to listen to her stories, to laugh with her, and to love her. Please sustain her life, and forgive me for waiting so long to see her."

Several anxious days had passed when the phone call from my mother reported what I had feared the most. "Honey, the doctors have informed us that there is nothing more they can do. Your grandmother's veins are collapsing. Another blood vessel in her brain has shattered. She isn't expected to live more than twenty-four hours. We were told to notify the family."

When I hung up the phone, I cried, "God, please, please give me back my grandma!" Consumed with remorse I scolded myself for taking my grandmother for granted. I assumed she would always be there when I could someday afford to go home.

I searched for an avenue so my prayers would reach heaven. Then I remembered Grandma Olga from church. We called her grandma because she loved and mothered us all. I often prayed with her and admired her strong faith and joyful countenance. My overwhelming desire to know my own grandmother had blossomed partly because of my relationship with her. I knew God would listen to Grandma Olga's prayers, so I called her.

After I poured out my heart, she calmly said, "Gena, you must surrender your grandma to Jesus. Give her up to God as Abraham did Isaac. It's what's best for your grandma that counts. God in His wonderful love knows how to work things together for good. Pray for her happiness, not yours."

It was painful to hear the truth, but I knew she was right. She prayed with me as I released my treasure to the Lord. "God, I'm sorry for my selfishness. Bless my grandmother and do what's best for her." I cried funeral tears. I felt sure the Lord would take my grandma home.

Now at peace, I managed to clean house and prepare a good meal for my family. I no longer wrestled, pleaded, or fretted. I continued to pray, "You are a wise and loving Father. You know my loss and my grief, but I ask You to fill those places in my life with Yourself. I love You most of all."

The phone's sharp ring startled me. Mom laughed as she declared, "Gena, a miracle has happened! Your grandma awoke from the coma and said, 'You know, I'm ready to go be with Jesus, but there's just one thing I regret. I haven't gotten to see my grand-baby, Gena.' Honey, how soon can you fly out to see her? I don't know how long she'll hold up, so hurry here!"

I screamed for joy, "God, You've given me back my grandma!" Every fiber of my being praised the Lord as I raced to pack for the trip. I flew south the next morning and by late afternoon was sitting at her bedside, holding her hand. We both wept.

"Precious girl, why have you stayed away so long?" she asked.

I just shook my head. "Grandma, I can't think of a good reason. You are so precious to me, and I'm grateful to be here at your side." She smiled and patted my hand.

For the next week, Grandma Carrie was alert and answered all of my carefully composed questions. Even though she was physically weak and couldn't lift her head from the pillow, she enjoyed every moment with her prodigal granddaughter.

Our heart-to-heart talks recaptured the years of separation and the identity I felt I lost because of the 2,500 miles that separated my grandmother and me. My Uncle Robert overheard Grandma talking about the farm days when her children were young. "Why, she hasn't been able to remember those stories in over twenty years!" he remarked.

I knew why Grandma's memory was so sharp; it was God's gift to me. She shared with me her jubilant acceptance of Jesus as her Lord and Savior at an old-fashioned tent revival when she was young. We laughed together over our common experiences of mothering and living. I finally realized my grandma knew, loved, and understood my life.

Every day I read Scripture to Grandma Carrie and prayed with her. On the last day of my visit, I read John 15:7 KJV to her. "If ye abide in me [Jesus], and my words abide in you, ye shall ask what ye will, and it shall be done unto you."

I said, "Grandma, I want to pray with you before I leave. What would you like to ask of the Lord? We'll agree in prayer together for your request."

To my surprise and delight she said, "I want God to heal me." I asked my younger sister, Paula, to join us in prayer. I placed my hand on Grandma's forehead as she closed her eyes to receive from her heavenly Father. I sensed His loving Presence in that room.

I began to pray, "Father...," but before I could speak another word, we felt the warm wave of His power flow between us. Tears brimmed Grandma's eyelashes, and I could barely utter the rest of the prayer. We knew that God had touched her.

As we lifted our heads, I asked, "Grandma, what kind of soup are you going to make?"

I left her room realizing that the entire week was a gift from God. Not only had I received my grandma's love, but the love of ten wonderful aunts and uncles. We shared our lives over meals. They affirmed me as part of their family.

Uncle George said, "Honey, don't stay away so long next time." Then he added, "How much did your trip cost?" When I told him, he quickly pulled out his checkbook to cover my expenses.

As I held out my hand to protest, I felt God's sweet assurance say, "I've provided for you in every way. Receive My gift with joy." I hugged my fatherly uncle and cried more happy tears.

As I flew back to Spokane, I marveled at God's love. Three weeks later, I received the news of Grandma's release from the hospital. Her complete recovery had baffled the doctors. She went home and made soup for her neighbors.

Seven months later on New Year's Eve, Aunt Loraine called to say that Grandma had peacefully passed away in her sleep. She died with a smile on her face. I looked up to God and smiled, too. I thought of Psalm 31:15 KJV, "My times are in thy hand...."

I face my future knowing that God can be depended upon. I am in His hands and know beyond a shadow of a doubt that His faithfulness endures to all generations. In surrendering my grandmother to Him, in His mercy He gave back to me what I had released to Him. I pray that I will always remember to keep my hands open in surrender to trust the goodness and wisdom of God.

If you remain in me and my words remain in you, ask whatever you wish, and it will be given you.

JOHN 15:7

Gena Bradford enjoys her profession as a public school teacher. She is also a gifted singer, songwriter, and freelance writer whose work has been published in various publications, including "Guideposts" magazine. She delights in recounting the stories of God's faithfulness. Gena and her husband, Jack, live in Spokane, Washington, and have four grown children.

10

MY MIRACLE BABY
by Marta Nelson

*A*lready a smoker by seventh grade, I quickly graduated to marijuana, alcohol, speed, and cocaine. At twenty-one I met my daughter's biological father. We didn't let Wayne's marital status hinder our decision to live together. When we first met, Wayne had been drug-free for a month. However, he soon returned to his crack cocaine addiction, and I went right along with him.

We made futile attempts to free ourselves from our bondage to narcotics. During these brief periodic efforts, Wayne had custody of his son and two daughters, and they lived with us intermittently during our precarious five-year relationship.

When Wayne's kids were in our custody, I took them to church every Sunday to appease my guilty conscience. I often got high Saturday night and would get up Sunday morning to take them to church. Attending church was my way of making amends to God and to my surrogate children for my drug-infested lifestyle.

When a neighborhood woman noticed me at church, she invited me to attend a women's retreat, which I willingly accepted. That weekend I invited Jesus into my heart and accepted Him as my Lord and Savior.

My life did not immediately change after I accepted Christ. A raging drug addiction and an immoral lifestyle continued to follow me for quite some time.

Shortly after the women's retreat, Wayne and I went on an extended, heavy drug binge. We were trying to run a traveling business that Wayne had started, so we spent most of our days on the road. Our drug addiction, however, consumed us, and we ended up losing everything, including our car. We traded off all of our material possessions to gratify our lust for drugs.

While living chaotically on the streets, I unexpectedly became pregnant. The fact that I conceived was a miracle in itself. I suffered from amenorrhea, a condition where menstrual cycles cease. I developed this condition as a result of severe malnourishment in my body, which was brought on by my extensive drug use. My eyebrow hair had fallen out, I hardly had any underarm or leg hair, and the hair on my head had thinned.

Even though I was pregnant, I couldn't break free from my enslavement to drugs. Wayne and I continued to wander from place to place, unable to conquer the vicious cycle of drug abuse.

In the midst of our drug binge and aimless road trips, my mom filed a missing person's report because she had not seen nor heard from me in over six months. Believing that I was dead, she gave all of my things away and emotionally tried to let me go.

While we were thought to be missing, Wayne and I lived on the streets in Southern California doing anything and everything to obtain money to support our drug habit. Arrested and released twice, my addiction continued to spin out of control.

We only ate once every three days—whatever we could steal. My occasional meal usually consisted of a small sandwich. No one could tell that I was five months pregnant with such an emaciated body.

Convinced that the drugs had poisoned my baby, I scheduled three different appointments during the first six months of the pregnancy to abort the fetus. Although I fully intended to follow through with the abortion, I never showed up for any of the appointments. I was always too high to drag myself to the clinic.

Because I did not have an official address, the police sent my criminal history to my mother's home in central California. Learning that I was still alive, she immediately called the police in Southern California to learn of my whereabouts. They were unwilling to divulge any information about me because of privacy laws. Although she begged for their assistance, their hands were tied and they refused to help.

An undercover police officer found me on the streets and bought me lunch. "It's my job to arrest you, but I really don't want to do that," he said. "You must have a home and a family I can send you to." Then he added, "Maybe I could help you find your family."

This would have been my third arrest. In the county I was in, a third arrest for being under the influence of drugs meant prison time, and babies born to pregnant inmates are taken from their mothers. Family and relatives aren't allowed to care for the children because officials do not want the babies to wind up in negligent hands again.

I told the officer about my family of twelve brothers and sisters, and he listened with a caring ear. After much encouragement from him, I agreed to return home to my family, and he agreed to get me there.

My mom was thrilled when the officer called and told her that he was putting me on a bus and sending me home. Since I would not leave without Wayne, he paid for Wayne's fare also. After promising the officer that I would stay on the bus until I reached my mother's home, we headed off on a seven-hour bus trip.

On the way home I thought, *Mom doesn't need to know I'm pregnant. I'll go home, clean up, and then get an abortion.* I was convinced that my continual drug use poisoned the baby. There wasn't any way my baby could be healthy. *Abortion is my only choice,* I thought.

Even though no one knew that I was carrying a baby, as soon as I stepped off the bus my mother gasped, "Oh my God, Marta, you're pregnant!" She had strong antiabortion convictions and would never allow me to go through with an abortion. My plans were quickly squelched.

The day after I came home, my mother contacted the California court system, this time as an advocate pleading for her daughter. "My daughter is home," she told the official. After their lengthy conversation, all charges against me were dropped. Giving impunity with the type of record that I had was unheard of in the court system that I was in. Yet, my case was dropped in its entirety.

Mom gave me tender care and attention during the next couple of months as she tried to help me get my life back together. However, shortly before I delivered my daughter, Marquita, I went back to Wayne with plans to work on our relationship.

I immediately returned to my old, familiar drug habits. I smoked cigarettes, marijuana, cocaine, and drank alcohol right up to the delivery of my precious baby. I downed a six-pack of beer the night before I gave birth and chain-smoked on the way to the hospital. Already focused on my next drug fix, I knew the moment I got out of the hospital and put the baby in my mom's arms, I would slip out to find drugs.

Because I was a known drug addict, I was assigned a doctor specializing in drug pregnancies.

Everyone was speechless when I gave birth to a beautiful, healthy baby girl weighing 6 pounds, 4 ounces. The hospital staff immediately tested Marquita for drugs because of my history. One doctor mentioned that one of the drug tests they used on me would show if cocaine had been in my system for the past three years. If drugs or alcohol were found in any of my baby's tests, Child Protection Services would take her away from me.

As the stunned doctor stared at his notes, he carefully reviewed the list of drugs I used throughout my pregnancy. Lab reports clearly showed that nicotine, cocaine, marijuana, and alcohol were in my system.

After examining my records in disbelief, he consulted two additional medical specialists. "Something is wrong here. The drugs are clearly in Marta's system," he said. "But every drug test on the baby is negative." Then he added, "This is medically impossible."

Marquita didn't have a trace of any foreign substance in her system. They couldn't take her from me! The doctors shook their heads in disbelief as they discussed my miracle baby.

How could God give me this perfect baby? I was amazed!

When the doctors left my room, I held Marquita in my arms and looked up to heaven. "God, if You can do this for her, You can do the same thing for me." A miracle was taking place in my life as well. At that moment, my desire for drugs instantly stopped!

I called my mom and said, "You better get a car seat. Marquita and I are coming home."

God transformed my life the day my miracle child was born. By the time Marquita was three months old, I'd read my Bible through three times. Leaving a life of drugs behind, I followed God's path for an abundant life. Ten years after her birth, my daughter continues to be a healthy, strong, and intelligent young lady. My family and I thank God for the wondrous miracle He did in our lives.

Before I formed you in the womb I knew you, before you were born I set you apart....

JEREMIAH 1:5

Marta Nelson is blessed with a loving husband and three children. She has served God for ten years and delights in her profession as a preschool teacher at Spokane Christian Academy in eastern Washington. Her daughter, Marquita, is a living testimony of God's unending love, grace, and mercy.

11

GOD DID NOT CREATE ME TO BE GAY!

by Sunny Jenkins

Like many children growing up in the sixties and seventies, I was raised in church and heard the Word of God preached every Sunday. Our family was very close, and I was especially close with my dad who had always wanted a boy. I was a tomboy while growing up and enjoyed masculine activities. I preferred fixing the car with my dad rather than fixing dinner with my mom.

When I was twelve, everything in my life changed when my mother ran off with a man from our church. My dad was devastated and blamed God for her leaving. He didn't realize at that time that Mom was not the only one who had abandoned our family. Shortly after my parent's divorce was final, Dad married an ungodly woman.

At thirteen, I got a summer job mixing cement to earn money to buy school clothes for my sister, Joetta, and me. I left home for good by the time I was fourteen. With no role models to follow, I tried to find my own way.

In addition to adjusting to my parents' divorce, I struggled with a growing attraction to girls. Because of my religious upbringing, I knew that homosexuality was a sin and often sat in church thinking, *God is going to strike me dead for having these thoughts!* I never had anyone I could talk with to share my feelings. I often asked myself, "Why would God let me have these feelings *if* they're so wrong?"

I began to actively participate in the homosexual lifestyle by the age of twenty. Then, for nearly 15 years, I proudly pursued this lifestyle. I didn't care who knew that I was gay. When introduced, I openly admitted it. If someone didn't like my lifestyle choice, I figured it was his or her problem. "This is who I am," I reasoned. "I was born this way."

I began drinking at the young age of thirteen and frequenting bars was something I enjoyed doing. I often spent $200 a night on alcohol and drugs. I was soon actively buying and selling drugs but eventually refined my drug habit to crank and marijuana. Drugs became a normal part of my daily routine, even while at work.

I tried to convince myself that my chaotic lifestyle was the best that life had to offer. In quiet moments, however, I believed a different story. Sometimes while sitting in the bar surrounded with friends, I felt utterly alone. I knew I wasn't the only one feeling that way as I often heard my friends cry, "Why can't somebody just love me?"

Inside, I knew the answer. *Someone can love you. His name is Jesus.* Though I knew what my friends and I needed, I didn't want to admit it to myself or to anyone else. I often lay awake at night fearing that I might die in my sleep and end up in hell. I told myself, "If I can just make it through the night, I'll be okay.

I occasionally called my childhood friend, Margaret, and unleashed my frustrations on her. "Stop praying for me!" I demanded. "Every time you pray things get worse!"

Margaret and my sister, Joetta, had prayed for me for 15 years. Eventually the women's Bible study at their church joined in with them. I hated the thought that people felt they needed to pray for me. Despite their prayers I delved deeper into homosexuality.

When my sister gave birth to her first child, I didn't want my niece to grow up and find out that her aunt was gay. Suddenly, my "out and proud" attitude changed. At the same time, bars no longer had the same appeal to me, so I stopped frequenting them. Although I wanted to be with my friends, life seemed empty. I thought, *I don't fit into the Christian world, nor do I fit into my world.*

Early one cold December morning in 1998 while I was getting ready for work, I felt as though a sledgehammer hit me in the chest. I thought I was having a heart attack. I broke out in a sweat and started to pass out. Somehow I was able to stay conscious until the feeling passed.

I went to a doctor and tests revealed that I had a heart condition called Wolff-Parkinson-White syndrome, a congenital heart arrhythmia.

Corrective surgery was immediately scheduled for mid-January. A tormenting fear gripped me while I waited for the surgery. I harbored an unshakable dread that if I went into surgery without Christ in my life, I wouldn't make it out of the operating room alive. Even with these agonizing thoughts, I was not ready to surrender my life to Christ.

It did not help that every night up until the surgery Margaret would call asking me if I had made things right with God. Furious at her question, I refused to let anyone push me into a decision I did not want to make. "I'm not going to say 'God help me,' and then go back to my old way of life," I fumed. "I already know everything you're telling me. Stop bothering me!"

But Margaret called again and again.

When I finally got a hold of myself and was ready to face surgery, the doctor unexpectedly postponed the procedure another week. I was furious; yet, I knew this was God's way of giving me one last chance. I felt as though I was pushed into a corner and was being forced to make a decision. I knew if I wanted to live, I had to choose God.

Pondering the price I would pay for choosing God, I realized that I would lose my gay friends, and I would have to stop drinking and taking drugs.

Marijuana and drug paraphernalia were stashed throughout my house. Beer filled the refrigerator and most of my drawers over-flowed with pornography and the phone numbers of many women. Turning my life over to Christ also meant that I would have to stop going to the gay pride picnics as well as quit the bar scene. I would also have to clean up my mouth and quit telling the crude jokes I so loved. My language could make a sailor blush.

How could I just walk away from everything I had known for the past 15 years? How could God demand that great of a sacrifice? No, I wouldn't make the choice!

Margaret persisted. I was smoking a joint on the eve of my surgery when she called again. "Have you made things right with God?" she asked.

"Margaret, this is who I am. God can't change me, and He can't change my feelings," I said. "God made me this way."

Not willing to give up, Margaret pressed me and finally convinced me to give God a try. On January 21, 1998, I somewhat reluctantly prayed with her to accept Jesus as my Lord and Savior.

After regaining consciousness following the surgery, I awoke knowing God was real and that He was working in my life. Even though I was an avid drug user for the past five years, my drug cravings vanished, and I never experienced any symptoms of withdrawal. I was no longer sexually attracted to women. After lovingly pursuing me for 35 years, God instantly and completely delivered me from the drugs and homosexuality that had dominated my life.

Margaret picked me up from the hospital. On the way home, we stopped at a Christian bookstore where I came across the book *Coming Out of Homosexuality* by Bob Davies and Lori Rentzel.[1] I quickly bought the book, and the truth became clear as I paged through it: God did not create me to be gay!

I am now grateful to the Christians who continued to pray for my salvation even when there weren't any visible signs that I would change. In the summer of 1998, I publicly declared my faith in Jesus before those faithful prayer warriors. The pastor who had unceasingly prayed many years for my salvation later baptized me as I symbolically laid down my old life and took on my new life in Christ.

> *The Lord is not slow in keeping His promise, as some understand slowness. He is patient with you, not wanting anyone to perish, but everyone to come to repentance.*

> 2 PETER 3:9

Sunny Jenkins lives in Chelsea, Oklahoma, where she actively works in the children's department of her church. She desires to share her testimony with teenagers, feeling that it can prevent them from going down the same path of despair and destruction that she traveled on.

12

PEGGY'S AND DONNA'S HEALING
by Pastor Martin Trench

In the late 1980s, I was a full-time evangelist on the staff of a church in Renfrew, Scotland, where I held monthly healing rallies. These rallies rapidly drew the largest attendance of any outreach of the church.

Before the healing rally, we served a free buffet meal, which created a wonderful opportunity to mix with the visitors and allowed them to see that we were "normal" people.

Each service began with a lively time of praise and worship. Because our visitors had already met us at the buffet, the arm-waving, hand-clapping fanatics they saw during the service didn't daunt them.

Being the most popular event in the church, members went out of their way to invite their friends and relatives. Month after month many people accepted Christ as their Savior, were baptized in the Holy Spirit, and received healing and deliverance. I always preached on faith-inspiring topics, which were followed by a powerful time of ministry and ended with a call for salvation.

I often received a word of knowledge concerning different people who were in need of physical healing. Sometimes God would give me very specific information about a situation, such as how long an individual had suffered from a particular illness. On occasion, He even revealed where a person was sitting.

On one occasion a Catholic woman named Peggy O'Dollan was in the congregation. It didn't appear that she was related to anyone in the church. She lived around the corner from the town hall where we met and had heard about the miracles that were taking place.

When Peggy came forward for prayer, she told me that for fourteen years she had suffered from spodilitis, a condition that affected her neck and back. Because she was unable to turn her head from side to side, her neck often became stiff. She wore a surgical collar and took a cocktail of eighteen prescription drugs every day to control the pain. Her condition prevented her from working in her garden and doing any housework.

I laid my hands on her head and boldly prayed for her complete healing. Nothing dramatic happened, and she returned home.

Peggy later told me, "I woke up the next morning in agony. I kept saying to myself, 'That young man said I would be healed, and I'm not. I could kill him!'"

However, two days after she had hands laid on her, she awoke with a surprising transformation. Peggy was totally and permanently healed! That day she went into her garden and diligently worked without any painful symptoms in her body. She then went into her house and hung curtains. Again, she didn't experience any pain in her neck or back.

Excited about her miraculous transformation, Peggy told many of her friends about her healing and invited them to attend the next healing rally with her.

Peggy soon brought Donna Jones, another Irish Catholic, to one of our healing meetings. When Donna came forward, it was obvious she needed God to heal the curve at the top of her back. I asked her, "What else do you want prayer for?" She then began to list off ailment after ailment.

I stopped her and said, "Let's just pray that God gives you a complete overhaul!"

No physical manifestation of healing appeared when we prayed. Donna, however, became a regular attendee of the rallies. She didn't get healed all at once but rather felt relief each time she received prayer. Ailment after ailment left her as she continued to have hands laid on her. Within a year the curvature in her spine completely disappeared, and she now stands straight and proud.

She told me, "I had to wear a surgical corset that contained steel bars in it just to keep me straight. My family used to jokingly call me a hunchback. God did a miracle for me just like he did for the woman who Jesus healed of the spirit of infirmity." (Luke 13:11.)

Peggy and Donna, two elderly close friends and sisters in Christ, both received incredible healing miracles in similar yet very different ways. They both had hands laid on them at the healing rallies. Peggy was healed instantly while Donna was healed gradually.

At the time of this writing, twelve years have passed since both women were healed; they are still healed today!

"But you will receive power when the Holy Spirit comes on you; and you will be my witnesses in Jerusalem, and in all Judea and Samara, and to the ends of the earth."

ACTS 1:8

Martin Trench is the senior pastor of River Ministries, a contemporary Christian church in Ayr, Scotland. Pastor Trench actively operates in the power of God and the gifts of the Holy Spirit. River Ministries' vision is based on Acts 20:20–to teach helpful principles, both publicly and in homes. The Trenches have three children: Jason, Josh, and Rebecca.

13

THE MIRACLE OF TRINITY
BROADCASTING NETWORK
by Paul Crouch, Jr.

"$\mathcal{B}$y faith, Abraham, when he was called to go out into a place which he should after receive for an inheritance, obeyed; and he went out, not knowing whither he went" (Heb. 11:8 KJV). After God had dealt with my parents, Paul and Jan Crouch, to start a Christian satellite network, they held on to this Scripture and to each other as they vowed to launch into the unknown.

Mom and Dad stepped out in faith with a thought, a prayer, and a Word from the Lord. In 1973 that was *all* they had. The money to operate a television station did not exist.

My parents diligently prayed for direction; in response to that prayer, the Lord reminded my dad of a fairly new TV station that had started on the air six months earlier.

Dad called the owner, Bill Myers, and inquired about the status. The transmitter for Channel 46 was located on Mt. Wilson, which was close to Los Angeles's main TV corridor. My father was floored when Mr. Myers explained that the station was no longer in service but had been forced to sign off the air.

Trying not to sound excited, Dad quickly made an appointment to discuss the possible acquisition of the station. A few days later, my parents purchased time on Channel 46 with an agreement to work on plans to purchase the entire station. They gulped as they signed the contract. They were committing to pay $10,000 a month for four evening hours on Channel 46.

At the same time, a member of our church and a partner in an industrial complex heard about their new venture. He explained that a computer firm had just moved out of the complex and suggested that the building might be the perfect home for the TV station.

The building contained large offices with smaller glassed-in rooms that could be used for studios. The electrical circuits and oversized air conditioners in the building were perfect for television. They signed the contract with three months of free rent.

For days everyone worked, scraping tile, hanging lights, and connecting equipment. The right people started to show up at the right time. A secretary walked in carrying a typewriter. Carpenters, electricians, and furniture movers miraculously happened by. God sent everybody with perfect timing.

Once when we needed to move a gas line, everyone formed a prayer circle. "Lord, we need a specialist for this job, and we don't have the money to hire him...." The words were barely spoken when Bill Crandall walked through the door. The patch on his uniform read "Southern California Gas Company." Bill closed valves, cut pipes, and made the way for the TV lights.

We were quickly approaching our scheduled sign on date, and the only thing that we needed was a microwave unit. This piece of equipment would transmit pictures and sounds from our newly remodeled studio in Santa Ana, California, to the transmitter on Mt. Wilson nearly 50 miles to the north.

We again prayed. "Lord, where do we find a microwave engineer?" Within minutes the phone rang. The caller? A microwave engineer! He and four other engineers arrived within hours.

The engineers worked for three days, but something kept blocking the signal. Not a glimmer of a picture came through. Nothing.

They tried everything. Finally in desperation they called the phone company, which provides microwave services. "Forget it!" the bad news began. "Either Whittier Hills or part of Mt. Wilson is blocking the transmission." The phone company had unsuccessfully tried sending microwave shots from several areas in Santa Ana in the past and had never been able to even get a dot of reception.

Time was running out! The station's FCC authority to remain off the air expired in two days. This was on a Saturday, and we had to be signed on by Monday. Our license could be lost if we did not meet our deadline.

Discouragement blanketed everyone involved in the project. It appeared as though my parents' dreams and plans were finished. Again they turned to the Lord.

My father then did something strange. He walked out of the building and around to the back. Matt and I silently followed him and watched as he climbed the ladder to the roof and the satellite dish. He wasn't even aware that we were watching. However, God wanted witnesses for the miracle that was about to be performed. Oh, how we needed a miracle.

Tears rolled down his face as he laid his hands on the curved steel of the microwave dish. "Father, You said that if we would have faith, even as a grain of a mustard seed, we could say to this mountain, be removed and be cast into the sea."

He dried his eyes and climbed back down the ladder. Matt and I watched as he rounded the studio's corner and bumped right into my discouraged, crying mother.

Dad told her, "I've just talked with my Father up on the roof, and everything is going to be fine!"

We returned to the studio. The engineers had already put in twelve hours that day and were packing up to leave. Dad asked the chief engineer if he would return the following morning.

"It's your money, Mr. Crouch," he said. "We'll give it one more shot, but personally I think it's a waste of time." Dad didn't tell him then, but we were virtually out of money.

We arrived at 8 A.M. sharp on Sunday morning. However, the tears and discouragement that filled the air the day before were gone. Instead, electricity saturated the room.

It took several minutes for the circuits to warm up, and the transformers hummed as final adjustments were made. An engineer on Mt. Wilson was on the phone with the chief engineer while we waited in the studio.

Suddenly, we heard a shout from across the room! "We've got it!" he yelled. "We've got the picture, and it's as clear as NBC!"

God moved a mountain for us. And for nearly 30 years, the TBN signal has been passing through that "cleft in the rock," sending Christian television around the world! God is awesome, and He loves to perform miracles![1]

> *...if you have faith as small as a mustard seed, you can say to this mountain, 'Move from here to there' and it will move. Nothing will be impossible for you."*

> MATTHEW 17:20

Paul Crouch, Jr., son of Paul and Jan Crouch, grew up in Christian television. His parents began Trinity Broadcasting Network (TBN) in 1973, the first Christian satellite network in the United States. Today, the network serves many satellites and stations throughout the world. Paul and his wife, Tawny, have three children.

14

A TALE OF TWO MIRACLES
by Laura Wagner

On March 23, 2001, while on my way to a horseback riding clinic in Wenatchee, Washington, the first of two miracles happened. Suddenly a person stepped off the curb and into the pathway of the car that I was following. The driver ahead of me slammed on his brakes to avoid hitting the pedestrian, and I, in turn, slammed on my brakes to avoid hitting him.

I was able to stop but was quickly jolted as the car behind me crashed into my car. After gaining my composure, I got out of the car to see if the other driver was okay. She was fine physically but was very nervous and shaky. Together we checked the damage to the cars.

To our amazement there wasn't a scratch on either car. She said, "I was going 35 miles per hour, and there should be more damage at that speed of impact. I don't understand how this could have happened."

"God is taking care of us; He's a loving and gracious Father," I told her before continuing on my way.

My second miracle took place that afternoon. During the riding clinic, the instructor separated the riders into three sub-groups. He called each sub-group into the arena one at a time and told us to form a line with our horses standing side-by-side.

He then called out one rider from the line. As the rider rode around the perimeter of the arena, the instructor told him or her what moves to perform and afterward critiqued his or her skills.

After I had completed my ride, the instructor said, "Go ahead and pull back into the lineup."

As I did this, my horse, Missy, reached down to scratch her face. At that moment, the ring on the running martingale rolled over the top of the knot, which holds the bit in place, and caused Missy's head to become bound in it.

Oh my, did she panic! "No, Missy, no!" I yelled as she pulled backward, apparently thinking that her head was restrained by the ground in front of her.

She began twisting her body to fight the monster that had her in its clutches. All eleven hundred pounds of her bodyweight fought to be freed from the pressure as she struggled frantically to get loose.

Imagine a horse being unable to straighten her front legs while her hind legs are backpedaling. This looks like a bucking bronco when the horse is in the air trying to buck a rider off. However, Missy still had all four feet on the ground.

In her struggle to free herself, she lost her balance. As her front feet began to lift off the ground, she began to fall. "Oh no!" swished through the spectators in the stands.

I could not control her fall as I, too, began to lose my balance. If I slipped from the saddle and onto the ground, the inevitable would happen. Missy would roll over backwards and on top of me. I would be crushed.

The only thing I knew that could save me was to yell "Jesus! Jesus! Jesus!" I fell off the horse, landing face down in the dirt.

There was nothing else to do but pray as Missy fell on top of me. She somehow succeeded in stopping her fall by landing on her knees, hovering over me. This kept her belly about a foot off the ground, just inches over my body.

The spectators watched in horror. They could only see my hands and feet sticking out from under her. I heard them cry, "Can you see her move? Is she hurt? Is she dead?"

As they watched this scene unravel, Missy suddenly composed herself. This is impossible for a horse to do. Anyone familiar with horses knows that when a horse gets off the ground after it has fallen, especially under extreme stress, it has no careful or calculated thought about its struggle to get up.

The spectators said it looked as though Missy was concerned about getting off the ground without injuring her master. She very carefully positioned her feet and body to get up from over the top of me and stood up using great care not to touch me with her shod hooves.

I believe the angels of the Lord saw to it that my horse landed on her knees that day. I also believe they instructed her to stay calm and to avoid any injury to me.

God was with me in a powerful way. I only had one small scratch on my arm as a result of the fall. And I was able to share my faith with everyone who witnessed this great miracle.

I'm sure that those who saw what happened will never forget this incident. And they will never forget the words that flowed from my lips in my time of peril—"Jesus! Jesus! Jesus!"

I will never stop thanking God for sparing my life that day. His plan for me did not include an untimely death. When danger comes, I never hesitate to call out to Him who is my refuge and my defense. I thank God for His abundant provision, which includes miraculous interventions in our lives.

> *I will sing of Your power; yes, I will sing aloud of Your mercy in the morning; for You have been my defense and refuge in the day of my trouble.*

PSALM 59:16 NKJV

Laura Wagner was raised in Southern California and has lived among the beautiful Cascade Mountains in the state of Washington for the past twenty-seven years. She has a wonderful husband, four grown children, and five grandchildren who have brought a lot of joy into her life. She surrendered her life to Jesus Christ in 1978.

A NOTE TO THE READER:

If you are a horse person, you will understand why Laura's story is a miracle. But if you do not know the way of the horse, Diana Clemons, horse trainer and handler, will convince you that this story is truly an awesome miracle. Here is her explanation.

> *As a horse trainer and handler, a story such as this where there is no injury to the horse or rider is truly amazing. By their very nature, horses are flight animals, similar to the deer family. They were designed by God to escape from their enemies. When they are afraid, their natural instinct tells them to run and get free from their predator.*
>
> *In this case the predator had trapped Missy's leg. A panicking horse is unbelievably dangerous and completely unpredictable. It is like a car with no driver, moving in reverse*

with the accelerator stuck into a crowd of people. Unless a horse has been trained to trust, her first response is always to escape danger.

I have seen this type of accident many times. A horse catches her foot in a halter or bridle, panics, and rears frantically with both horse and rider going over backwards. Many riders have been killed or seriously injured in this type of fall.

I have never heard of anyone falling completely under a horse and not being injured. Because of the shape of a horse's anatomy, if its four legs are tucked under her, there is approximately seven inches of space where her belly does not touch the ground.

Astounding as well is the fact there was no injury to Laura as Missy rose to her feet. Rising from the ground to a standing position is very awkward, even to a calm, quiet horse. I always warn students at my ranch to be very careful around a horse getting to its feet because bringing eleven to fourteen hundred pounds from the ground to a standing position is very precarious.

A horse must literally throw her front feet forward and out in front of her, then rock back on her hind end and use her powerful back legs to launch into a standing position. The fact that this frightened horse did not crush her rider with scrambling feet is astonishing. Amazing as well is the fact that this horse didn't move after it rose, but stood still.

Had God not had His hand sovereignly on Laura, I believe she would now be dead or seriously maimed. God truly protected both Laura and Missy in their time of trouble.

Diana Clemons is the owner and head trainer of Northwind Stables, Inc., located in Rathdrum, Idaho.

15

MIRACLE ON WHITE RIVER
by David Wagner

$\mathscr{I}$t was the middle of May and Memorial Day weekend was quickly approaching. My first wife, Bina, and a group from the church had decided they wanted to take a canoe ride that Saturday. Being a cautious person, I wasn't convinced that canoeing was such a good idea.

My experience with canoes was limited to lakes; I didn't have any experience with them on rivers. The church group had picked the White River for our fun adventure. Several canoes had been borrowed from a local kids' camp and all the plans had been set for the canoe trip and picnic. We were scheduled to leave early in the morning.

I didn't want to be a "wet blanket," but for some reason I couldn't shake the heaviness I felt about this canoe outing. Something bad was going to happen. I just knew it.

I had surrendered control of my life to the Lord a few years prior and sincerely wanted to do whatever He asked of me. I sometimes found it difficult to know the difference between the leadings of God and my own conservative, logical way of thinking. This was one of those times. I wasn't sure whether it was God or my own fears, but I was certain that we should not go canoeing. The night before the trip, I told Bina that we should stay home. She wanted me to sleep on it and see if I felt the same way in the morning.

I awoke Saturday morning still feeling the same dread I felt the day before. As I prayed in my time alone with the Lord, I experienced what I describe as a daydream. I saw myself struggling to push my six-year-old daughter, Kiersten, up and out of fast-moving water. I was drowning. The water was pulling me down, and I was incapable of fighting against it. The images frightened me so much that I told my wife I was not going on the canoe trip.

As I ate breakfast, however, I changed my mind. I decided that I would go along but only to ferry the car from where they put the canoes into the landing several miles down river. This would make the logistics simpler for everybody.

When we got to the river, we saw that it was running quite high with a lot of debris floating in the strong current. The fast-moving, gray-green water was a result of the runoff of the spring thaw from the mountains. My logical thinking knew that this was not going to be a fun trip. Our group leader, however, told us he had called ahead and discussed the river conditions with the forest ranger. The ranger told him that he felt we would not have any problems, even though only two canoes would have experienced people in them.

That's when my logical mind relented, and I decided to go along. I don't know exactly what caused me to change my mind. It could have been that I didn't want to spoil things for the others and trusted the ranger more than my own logic.

I wasn't sure that what I saw during my prayer time was God showing me what was about to happen or if it was simply an over-active imagination. Or maybe I was compelled by "manly pride" to protect my family instead of looking like a wimp in front of my daughter. Whatever the reason, I helped to unload the canoes and get them into the water.

The experienced canoeists were in the first two canoes, we were third, and three more canoes filled with inexperienced folks were behind us. Bina was in the front of our canoe with Kiersten in the middle. I was at the rear.

After we pushed off, I immediately knew that this excursion was not going to go well. The current was very strong, and I saw a logjam extending out from the left bank. I told Bina to paddle hard to the right. As we cleared the first jam, we saw a second logjam jutting out from the right bank immediately downstream.

I then instructed Bina to paddle hard to the left, but it was too little too late. We ran straight into a narrow gap created by two small logs. After the impact, the swift current caused our canoe to roll over, and we toppled into the cold water.

After surfacing, the three of us hung onto the inverted canoe. Kiersten and I were on the left side, and Bina was on the right. Kiersten tried to climb up onto the canoe to escape the cold water but that made it impossible for Bina and me to hold onto it. I told her to hold on tight and wait until we could get to land.

At first I didn't notice how cold the water was. I had too many other things to occupy my mind. I saw another logjam directly ahead of us jutting out from the left bank. The log we were about to hit was nearly 36 inches in diameter with half of it above the surface of the water. When we hit the log, the canoe went under water. I was able to grab Kiersten and hoist her up onto the log. Bina was already there to help.

That's when I began to notice the cold. I knew we had to get out quickly. We couldn't last long in the cold water. If we stayed in the water much longer, we also risked getting hit by the other canoes.

Just as I was ready to climb out of the water and onto the log, I felt our submerged canoe begin to press my legs against a log and pull me under. I remembered my "dream" from earlier that morning and realized that God *had* given me a vision. It was *not* my conservative thinking, but God had tried His best to warn me about this situation. Unfortunately, I failed to recognize and listen to His "still, small voice."

As I pondered the possibility of drowning, I felt total peace knowing that my family was safe and that I would soon be face-to-face with my Lord.

Suddenly the canoe released its grip on my legs. I quickly climbed up onto the log and checked Kiersten who was shivering from cold and shock. There was nothing we could do for her except for Bina to hold her close for warmth.

I looked upstream in search of the rest of our party and saw that another canoe had also capsized. I could see two heads sticking out of the water holding onto the canoe as it approached our log. When their canoe hit us, the lady in front was able to climb up onto the log. The man, however, had become pinned between the canoe and the side of the log. He was trapped under water. We could see his arm reaching up trying to pull himself free.

I searched for something to use as a tool. Finding a short, stout log I returned to the canoe and tried to pry it free. It quickly became evident that my efforts were futile.

Just then I felt a tap on my shoulder. The young man who had been trapped in the canoe was suddenly next to me. He explained that as he realized he was helpless to do anything and would soon be in the Presence of God, he suddenly found himself on top of the log next to me.

All of the canoes with inexperienced people capsized that morning. Two of the canoes were crushed so deeply into the logjam that they were never retrieved. All of the capsized people were able to climb onto logs until help arrived. Nobody was killed or injured that day.

We learned many things that morning about our loving Savior and ourselves. He truly does care for His children, even when we fail to heed His warnings and choose to do foolish things.

The angel of the Lord encamps around those who fear him, and he delivers them.

PSALM 34:7

David Wagner is a semiretired mechanical engineer living in Leavenworth, Washington, with his second wife Laura. David accepted Jesus as Lord at age thirty-one. His hobbies include steam powered logging and modeling history. He is the editor of "Safety Valve Letters" for his local newspaper.

16

MISSION IMPOSSIBLE
by Laurie Klein

The invitation to lead a worship weekend in former East Germany lay on the table stacked with other prayer concerns. My husband, Bill, and I knew this mission, should we choose to accept it, involved language study. Easy for him; he knew some German. For me? Impossible.

My past experiences proved that any vocabulary stashed in my brain would self-destruct the moment I needed it the most. I had squeaked through high school Spanish and only passed college French because I was the professor's student aide, and she liked me. This brain was now three times older. *What* was God thinking?

When I prayed about going to Germany, I only listened for an answer with one ear open. However, God resoundingly made it as clear as a bell that we were to go. Even with one ear closed, I couldn't ignore His direction.

Within a week Bill and I enrolled in weekly German classes. Our instructor, Inge, was bright, funny, patient, and passionate. Over time, she helped us to translate choruses, Scripture readings, and many exercises that I would use to teach a devotional journaling workshop.

When at last we departed, I begged God to bless my efforts. After all, this was His idea. I would never send a language dunce and daughter of a World War II vet to Dresden, a fairytale city that was ravaged during that war.

For the first half of my workshop, a wonderful woman named Christiane translated for me. Eager to participate, she scribbled as fast as she could in between interpreting my directions. I bumbled ahead, clutching Inge's 4 x 5 color-coded cards.

Perched for a time in the courtyard garden, my class created parables from nature, composed psalms, and harnessed childhood memories for poems. These were typical exercises, nothing earth-shaking, or so I thought.

After three hours, I closed with prayer. No one moved. Assuming I'd muddled my verb tenses, I tried again. "It's over, friends."

Silence. I caught a friend's eye. She shrugged. More prayer then, I reasoned. I moved from person to person, laying hands on each of them. Only God knows what I prayed. My German is abysmal, but I can be fluent in love.

Twenty minutes passed. Thirty. Except for the tears, they sat as if spellbound. Thirty-six beautiful, breathing statues. I begged God for understanding.

Then a flash of insight came. As it was in the book of Genesis, when the Spirit of God hovered over the darkness before He spoke light into being, these people survived the dark wilderness of communism. They were never able to express their feelings without jeopardizing everything they had, their career, their family, and their future. This was the first time they were able to pour out their hurts and express whatever was in their hearts. The Spirit of the living God breathed on them, and light shone in their hearts.

"...Everything is possible for him who believes."

MARK 9:23

Laurie Klein adores her family and her ongoing studies in art, writing, theatre, music, and movement. She has authored the praise chorus "I Love You, Lord." If granted three wishes today, she would choose to love well, live in the moment, and the third...sorry, it's a secret!

17

"GOD HEALED HER WHEN YOU PRAYED"

by Pastor Steve Valentine

While ministering in Seattle at a family camp for our church, I was asked by a pastor friend to go with him to a local hospital to pray for the newborn infant of a couple in his church. The tiny baby was born without kidneys. When we arrived, we asked the nurse if we could pray for her.

"Do whatever you wish," she said. "This child is not going to live."

After scrubbing up, we were able to lay our hands directly on the infant. We prayed for her through the holes in the sides of the incubator where she was hooked up to all kinds of life support machines. Afterward we left.

The next day I returned to my home in Missoula, Montana. I had forgotten about this incident until fourteen years later when I was speaking at another family camp in Oregon. After one of my sessions, a man came over to me and introduced himself.

"Do you remember praying for a baby who was born fourteen years ago without kidneys?" he asked.

"Yes I do."

"I'm her dad," he said.

I wasn't sure what to say next.

Then he asked, "Would you like to meet her?"

"She's alive?"

"Yes. God healed her when you prayed for her," he replied.

"Was she healed instantly or did she undergo surgery? How was she healed?" I questioned.

"There was no need for surgery!" he declared. "Shortly after you prayed, her body began to function normally. The doctor told me he couldn't explain it but must have misdiagnosed her condition. They took her off of the life support systems, and she was released from the hospital soon after."

My wife, Kay, and I were then introduced to a beautiful fourteen-year-old girl. My first question was, "Can you go to the bathroom?"

Puzzled at my question, she answered, "Yes."

Her dad then told her I was one of the men who had prayed for her when she was born. My wife and I cried tears of joy at the faithfulness of God. He is so merciful to us and to the nurse who got to see this baby leave her care, healthy and whole. What an amazing Christ we serve!

"Have faith in God," Jesus answered.

"I tell you the truth, if anyone says to this mountain, 'Go, throw yourself into the sea,' and does not doubt in his heart but believes that what he says will happen, it will be done for him."

MARK 11:22,23

Pastor Steve Valentine is the founding pastor of Clark Fork Christian Center, Missoula, Montana. Pastor Valentine and his wife, Kay, have pastored for 24 years and have established churches throughout the United States and Mexico.

18

GOD EVEN CARES ABOUT WARTS
by David White

I had just graduated from high school and was working on the family farm through the summer prior to going to college. During that summer tiny bumps began to develop on the right side of my neck two inches below my jaw. When the bumps first appeared, I didn't give them much thought. They weren't painful and there were only a few of them, so I assumed they would go away on their own.

As summer ended and college was about to begin, the bumps had not gone away but had worsened. They multiplied and grew to the size of a metal-headed pin. These strange bumps made it difficult to shave. When shaving with an electric razor, the razor would grab and tear the small ones off. If I used a regular razor, the blade shaved most of the bumps off. It usually took ten minutes to stop the bleeding, and the bumps always returned.

When college started I roomed with my pastor's son, who was two years older than me. Although he was raised in a Christian home, he had turned away from God.

By this time the bumps covered a two-inch area of my neck and had become embarrassingly noticeable. Not only were the unsightly bumps physically irritating, but they also caused me to become extremely self-conscious. After several months of frustration, I was desperate to find an avenue to rid myself of them so I finally made an appointment to see a doctor.

The doctor diagnosed the bumps as warts and said he could not treat them because they were so numerous and small in size. Leaving me with discouraging words, he said, "The warts probably won't go away. In fact, it's possible they will just keep growing. I just don't know."

Being eighteen and single, the thought of going through the rest of my life with warts on my neck only increased my anxiety. If the warts continued to grow and multiply, I knew my dating life would come to a fast end.

Desperate to find an answer, I turned to prayer. I knew the Bible said that if I asked God for something, I would receive it. (John 16:24.) So I asked and I asked but didn't get any results.

After a month of daily petitioning God to heal me, I began to make excuses for why the warts remained. *They're just warts,* I thought. *It's not really life threatening or serious in any way. Maybe God doesn't want to heal me. Maybe my Christian walk with God isn't what it should be and that's why I'm not getting healed.*

None of the excuses seemed right to me, so I continued to pray the same prayer every night. "God, heal me of these warts. Please remove them from my neck."

One afternoon while I was in the tub, my roommate came into the bathroom, and we started talking about the Lord. Because he was a pastor's son, he knew a lot about God, but he didn't live what he knew. We talked about the fact that he was not living for God.

He knew about the warts on my neck and was aware that I had been asking God to heal them. Looking up at my roommate with soap covering my face I said, "Do you see these warts on my neck?

"Yes" he answered with a questioning expression.

"God is going to heal me of these warts. I don't know how or when, but God is going to heal me."

I reached into the tub and splashed water on my face to rinse the soap off. As my hand slid down my face over my neck, I realized that almost all of the warts were gone.

Looking up at my roommate with surprise, I saw his eyes widen and his mouth drop open. We witnessed a miracle. The few remaining warts completely vanished within two days and have never returned.

If God cares enough to heal an eighteen-year-old kid of warts, just imagine what else He wants to heal!

Jesus went through all the towns and villages, teaching in their synagogues, preaching the good news of the kingdom and healing every disease and sickness.

MATTHEW 9:35

David White is a fourth generation wheat farmer. He became a Christian in 1979 in a small town of 600. David and his beautiful wife, Diane, have five children and continue to live on and work the family farm.

19

ANGEL IN THE SNOWSTORM

by Therese Marszalek

*L*eaving the Honeywell office parking lot in Minneapolis, I joined the thousands of snow-covered cars inching their way through an unexpected blizzard. Although strangers, we all shared the common goal of reaching the safety and warmth of our own homes. It was by far the worst snowstorm I had witnessed in 20 years. Realizing I was going to be late to pick up my young son, James, I silently prayed for grace with his babysitter.

The wheels of my little red Chevy spun as I pulled onto the freeway, entering an endless line of cars. I grumbled when I noticed the red "check engine" light flashing its irritating eye at me. My frustration rose as I recalled having my company car serviced just the week before, yet the stubborn "check engine" light continued to flash intermittently.

While concentrating on keeping sight of the car ahead of me, an obnoxious sound erupted from under the hood, threatening an already challenging trip home. I regretted the decision I had made earlier in the week to delay scheduling an appointment for the car to be rechecked. My demanding schedule could not afford to squeeze in one more distraction.

The irritating noise from under the hood demanded increasing attention and made me wonder if my car would survive the homeward journey at all. Thankful the windows of other cars were closed, I knew the undeniable grinding noise would attract embarrassing stares. Although the quickly mounting engine trouble cried for immediate attention, finding my way to a service station in the middle of this ferocious storm was not an option.

The blizzard raged fiercely, making it impossible to clearly make out the cars in front of or behind me. To pull off the road would mean putting myself in harm's way. After all, who would possibly offer help at a time like this? Anyone on the road during this storm was focused on his own survival.

Almost halfway to my coveted destination, a loud explosion erupted from under the hood. The steering wheel became hard to fight, and I realized that the power steering was gone. With only enough power to inch over to the side of the freeway, my wounded car crawled out of the slow-moving ribbon of cars.

Then there was silence. The obnoxious grinding noise was now gone, only the eerie howling wind swept across the freeway.

What am I going to do now, Lord? I fretted, as my heart raced in my chest. *I can't get out of the car in this storm. I'm late to pick up James, and I can't even let his babysitter know the car has broken down.* Overwhelmingly helpless, I closed my eyes and sighed, "Help me, Lord."

Slowly opening my teary eyes, I peered into the foggy rearview mirror and noticed a small red speck at a distance behind my car. Watching the red form increase in size I realized a person was running along the freeway in my direction. *How can this be?* I thought. *Where did that person come from?*

As she neared the car, I rolled down the window to find a pleasant young woman in a fluffy red coat standing at my side. Her warm expression indicated no concern about standing on a crowded freeway in the midst of a monstrous storm.

"What can I do to help you?" Her welcome smile instantly calmed my racing heart.

After filling her in on my diagnosis of a blown engine, she offered to give me a lift to a service station and phone.

The brave stranger instructed me to wait in my car. Her red form disappeared once again into the raging storm. Minutes later, her royal blue car pulled over in front of me as she motioned me to get in. Feeling emotionally numb, I willingly hopped in the front seat, kicking the snow off my heels.

Anxious thoughts whirled through my mind as we drove to the service station. Being lost in thoughts of my pending dilemma, I didn't notice the silent peace that saturated the atmosphere in the car.

Without any instruction from me, my driver took the next exit and found the nearest service station. I thought to myself, *She must be from around here.*

As she pulled up to the door, I quickly exited the car, already focused on the next task at hand. Almost forgetting to thank my Good Samaritan for her kindness, I spun around before opening the service station door. The car was nowhere to be seen.

Speechless, I wondered how my rescuer could have disappeared so quickly. I searched every direction yet saw only blowing snow and cars spinning their wheels. My kind rescuer had vanished.

Who was that woman? I thought. Straining my eyes and looking in every direction once again, I suspected I may have been dreaming, but the biting wind and icy snow hitting my face reminded me that this surely was not a dream.

After making arrangements to tow my wounded car, a kind service station worker drove me to the babysitter's home and then delivered us to our front door. With a sigh of relief, I welcomed the safety and comfort of my warm home.

Sinking into an easy chair with a steaming cup of coffee, I quietly pondered my journey through the snowstorm. *Who was the nameless woman who appeared as quickly as she had disappeared? Who was the kind servant who radiated such peace? Who was the mysterious rescuer who was willing to make such a sacrifice for a perfect stranger?*

Tears welled in my eyes as God brought to my remembrance that in the middle of my helpless trial, I had called out to Him for help. Filled with gratitude, I realized that my angel in the snowstorm was one sent by God. Once again, He poured out His everlasting mercy and proved His faithfulness.

Without even knowing it, I had been in the midst of a servant of the Most High. God's special messenger had been sent to help in my time of need.

He will call upon me, and I will answer him; I will be with him in trouble, I will deliver him and honor him.

PSALM 91:15

Therese Marszalek is a freelance writer who authored the book Breaking Out *and is the coauthor of this anthology. Her calling in the body of Christ is to publish and teach hope and healing through Jesus Christ and His Word. Therese and her beloved husband, Tom, have three growing and active children.*

20

THE DEAD MAN LIVES
by Troy Stone

*I*t was a beautiful summer evening as my friend, Pam, and I drove through Spokane, Washington, heading back to Coeur d'Alene, Idaho, on Interstate 90. The full moon lit up the hills and valleys like daylight. We were enjoying the view while reminiscing about the great party we had just left.

We both noticed a fellow in the right lane ahead of us weaving back and forth on a Ninja-type motorcycle. He was riding with his head down low over the bike.

"Pam, that fella looks like he's either asleep or drunk," I said.

"Yeah, he's going to get himself hurt if he doesn't stop weaving." Just then, the bike veered into the left lane, over the shoulder, and onto the grass median. It looked as though he was driving down the middle of the road on purpose.

"Dear Lord, protect him," I cried.

All of a sudden his head popped up.

"I think he just woke up," Pam said.

We could see that he was wearing nothing but a white t-shirt, jeans, boots, and a black, full-faced helmet.

Sensing the danger he was in, he tried to get back onto the freeway. However, he overcorrected his bike and found himself weaving back and forth between lanes.

"He's going too fast! He's going to get killed!" Pam squealed.

"He's gonna wreck," I said, slowing my car and knowing the imminent danger.

As those words were uttered, the bike began to swerve and slide. It began to flip end over end five, six, seven times carrying the rider with it. It finally slid to a stop with the bike on top of the rider.

I slammed on my brakes and careened sideways on the pavement in front of the accident victim, stopping traffic so it would not cause more damage to the man.

Pam and I jumped out of the car and ran to him. He was twitching and turning on his back. We lifted the bike off of him with the help of other motorists who had stopped to give aid. I lifted the visor so I could see his face. Blood oozed from his eyes and nose. He was unconscious.

"Oh, dear Lord!" I said. "Please help this man!"

Two ribs stuck through his blood stained and tattered t-shirt. One leg looked as though it had a compound fracture, and he was lying on his right arm, which was bent behind his head.

Pam pulled back and began to freak out. "He's gonna die! Do something, Troy," she screamed.

I was trying to comfort the man when he stopped twitching and lay deathly still.

A man came running up to us. "I'm a doctor. Get out of my way, so I can look at him." He checked his pulse and exclaimed, "He's gone."

"Oh no, dear Lord, no!" we both cried.

"Call 911, call an ambulance," I heard someone say. Another passerby brought a blanket to cover his body.

Something inside of me rose up and caused me to step to the front of the dead man. I stopped the blanket before it reached his face. I knew it wasn't time for him to die. I pulled the blanket back and placed my hands on the helmet still on his head. Pam looked at me, knowing what I was about to do.

"Father, in the Name of Jesus, I ask You to spare this man's life. Please bring him back to life." I rebuked the angel of death, saying, "It's not time for this man to leave this place. He has work to do for the Lord! Now, Satan, get your hands off of him. He is healed in the name of Jesus!"

I prayed for less than a minute before hearing ambulance and police sirens. Within seconds the police and paramedics were at his side. Suddenly, the man who was declared dead only minutes before gasped for air. He looked at me as though saying, "What's going on? Why am I here?"

Then pain overcame him, and he began to scream and moan in agony. The medics removed his helmet and placed a brace around his neck. They tended to him with IV's and carefully laid him on the gurney.

Pam and I followed him to the ambulance. His hand had fallen off of the gurney. I gently grasped it and held it until he was placed in the ambulance. His eyes, filled with tears, never left mine. Although he could not speak, I knew he realized what had happened. He knew that he had been prayed back to life.

The attendants loaded the gurney into the ambulance, closed the door, and sped off to the hospital.

"Thank You, Lord, for letting him know that You have healed him," I told God.

Back in my car, Pam and I praised and thanked God during the next couple hours of our long drive. We were ecstatic that this man was given a second chance at life. Pam was never sure that God was really who He said He was. That night she gave her life to the Lord.

When we arrived at Pam's home in Idaho, we called the hospital to check on his condition. "He's recovering very well. I expect that he will be released from the hospital in three or four days," the nurse said. "It's a miracle that he's alive!"

Then he went up and touched the coffin, and those carrying it stood still. He said, "Young man, I say to you, get up!"

The dead man sat up and began to talk, and Jesus gave him back to his mother.

LUKE 7:14,15

Troy Stone lives in Maui, Hawaii, with his wife, Lynette, and daughter, Jessica. He and his brother, Tory, own and manage Maui Brothers Activities and Tours. Troy has served the Lord since he was fifteen. He is a writer and musician and loves to race motorcycles.

21

A DIVINE APPOINTMENT

by Sara O'Meara

*I*n 1972 I learned that my body was riddled with cancer. Five doctors confirmed that the cancer had spread to every gland in my body and all agreed that I had less than three months to live.

You can't imagine how I felt when I was told that my life was going to end so soon. Having two little boys to raise by myself, the death sentence was quite a blow.

While watching television in my hospital room after the surgery, an advertisement flashed on the screen for an upcoming appearance by the noted healer, Kathryn Kuhlman. In the commercial she spoke directly to me when she said, "Be at the Shrine Auditorium in Los Angeles this Sunday because you need a miracle."

I thought, *I'm going to be there.*

I was brought up Presbyterian. In fact, my best friend, Yvonne, and I had met as Presbyterian Sunday school teachers. I did not know anything about supernatural healing or healing services. To me, these were "holy roller" activities, and people just made a lot of noise during the service. I decided that I didn't care. I knew I must attend Kathryn Kuhlman's meeting.

Making it to her meeting, however, required divine intervention. I wasn't supposed to leave the hospital until four days after she was scheduled to appear at the Shrine. I insisted on getting out of the hospital before that Sunday. I knew I *had* to be at that meeting.

I was very weak when I left the hospital. An incision on one side of my body was eighteen inches long. Dissolvable stitches did not exist at the time. Clamps held my incision closed. Because of the extensive surgery, the doctor told me I would have to go home and stay in bed with minimal movement. If I wouldn't agree to his instructions, he wouldn't release me from the hospital. I promised to obey his instructions.

Someone once said promises are made to be broken. I had an appointment with destiny and nothing was going to stop me.

When Sunday arrived Yvonne picked me up and drove me to the Shrine Auditorium. Although I was in pain and discomfort, I insisted on going to the meeting regardless of how I felt.

After walking from the car to the auditorium, I was bleeding profusely and had become extremely weak. Yvonne asked, "Do you think you're going to make it?"

"I *have* to get inside," I told her.

But when I reached the entrance, the doors were closed. The ushers said that every chair had already been taken, and they would not let me in. After all I had gone through to get to the meeting, their discouraging words floored me.

Suddenly, the door opened and a woman came outside. I was surprised to see another friend of mine. She had come outside to get a sweater from her car because it was cold in the auditorium. Shocked to see me, she said, "What in the world are you doing here, Sara?"

"I'm not feeling well, and I had hoped to get into the meeting," I said. "But there are no seats left."

Without hesitation, she responded, "You take my seat, and my husband will give his seat to your friend."

Usually I would have said no, but instead I said, "I'd love to."

The seats were at the top of the first balcony in the last row. By the time I had climbed the endless steps, I was completely exhausted.

When the meeting started, I felt as though I was being lifted up and knew that I was either dying, hallucinating, or that something fabulous was happening to me.

Kathryn was speaking when suddenly she stopped and said, "There's a wonderful healing of cancer in the balcony. It's a girl who has cancer throughout her body."

I knew at once that something wonderful was happening to me, and I was thrilled. Not sure that Kathryn was talking about me, I prayed, "God, if You're touching me, please let me know it in a very real way."

Kathryn continued talking until she stopped abruptly again. "You'll know that you're being healed," she said boldly. "It feels as though a thousand needles are going through your body at once."

It was true! I felt as though I had grabbed hold of an electrical current. While what felt like a thousand volts of electricity flowed through my body, I knew that God was touching me.

Unbeknownst to me at the time, the entire row of people sitting next to me had been knocked down from the surge of super-natural power. A woman who was sitting in the same row told me about the remarkable experience after the meeting.

Kathryn Kuhlman continued talking, then stopped again and said, "The girl sitting in the last row of the first balcony in a red dress—stand up," she commanded. "You are healed."

Although I knew she was talking to me, I couldn't stand up because I was shaking so hard. The ushers approached me and said, "Aren't you the one that's been healed?"

"Yes," I answered.

"Well, go down and give your testimony," they insisted.

I paused with hesitation. I didn't want to go to the platform. I thought, *Go down in front of all these people and tell them what has happened? This is too personal.*

A quiet but strong voice inside of me said, "You mean I would do this for you, and you won't give Me the glory?"

As I rose from my seat, supernatural energy soared through my body. I felt like a different person. The bleeding had stopped, and I literally raced down the steps toward the platform.

As I walked down the aisle on the main floor, I saw many other people who had also been healed and were anxious to get up on the stage. I thought, *Oh good, she'll never get to me because there are so many others. I'll just meander on down.*

Kathryn called to me and said, "You in the red dress, get up here! The glory of God is all over you!" She was very dramatic. "Get up here and tell what God has done for you. He has saved you for a very special purpose."

I stepped on the stage and shared my testimony. I told Kathryn that while I was sitting in my seat, a pink cloud floated toward me from the right side of the auditorium and surrounded me. I have never seen such a cloud since that time. As I shared every detail of my story, the people in the auditorium were very quiet. They knew my healing had taken place.

After the meeting, I was scheduled to see the doctor the next morning. My dear Yvonne took me to the appointment and sat in the waiting room while I saw the doctor. I hadn't been in the examining room very long when the doctor came flying out of the room and said to her, "You have the craziest friend I've ever seen. She's completely healed! There's nothing there!"

After the doctor examined me, I was able to tell him about my miracle. He's never been the same since, nor have I.

The date of my healing, February 20, was a very special date not only because God had given me a second chance in life, but also because it was the birthday of my older son and the date that Kathryn Kuhlman would be taken home to God years later.

I worked with Kathryn Kuhlman in the healing ministry until her death and am living proof that God is still performing miracles on the earth.[2]

He heals the brokenhearted and binds up their wounds.

PSALM 147:3

Sara O'Meara, formerly a Hollywood starlet, cofounded Childhelp USA®, a national nonprofit organization dedicated to meeting the physical, emotional, educational, and spiritual needs of abused and neglected children. Sara is married to Robert Sigholtz, Ph.D. She has a son and two stepdaughters. Another son, Charles, died in an auto accident in 1988.

22

A MESSAGE FROM HEAVEN
by Margie Davis

*M*y oldest son, Donny, came into this world in 1960 shortly after I had turned 18. He was special to me from the first time I held him in my arms. As he grew older, he became increasingly protective over his younger brothers, Mike and Scott, and even more so over his sister, Tami.

Donny created crazy nicknames for his loved ones and always brought laughter wherever he went. He called his grandmother "Ethel," knowing it made her mad. He would tease her, saying that he was going to pick her up on his Harley and take her to Reno. I could only imagine Donny with a do-rag on his head and Grandma perched on the back of his Harley, hanging on for dear life.

Family meant more to Donny than anything. His nieces and nephews were crazy about him. He was always willing to help strangers. Donny was generous to a fault and reached out to every needy person that crossed his path. Everyone—family, friends, and strangers—commented about his good heart.

Donny never married. He became a drywall finisher when he was fourteen and did finishing work across the country until his death in 2002. Donny liked being on the move. We never knew where he'd call from or when he might show up unexpectedly. Wherever he called from, he'd say, "Don't worry, Mom, I'm okay." But I did worry; I worried about him always.

On March 2, 2002, while Donny was walking along the railroad tracks in Ventura, California, a train caught him by surprise. He tried to escape the train's path but didn't jump off the tracks in time. The train struck my precious son and killed him instantly.

At his funeral, my daughter Tami tucked a heart-shaped rock in Donny's grave. Her fourteen-year-old son, Jesse, had given her this unique treasure when he was only four. Tami said that because Donny's heart was as solid as a rock, she wanted him to have this cherished heart.

Since my son's death, I've asked the Lord to heal the pain of my loss. The grief from losing Donny has been so deep that I've often wondered if I could go on with my life. Knowing that Donny won't call me anymore or show up at the door is unbearable at times.

One day about three weeks after Donny's death, my husband and I were planting flowers in the garden. Saturated in grief, I sobbed so hard I could hardly see. My flowing tears watered my newly planted flowers. Looking to the heavens I cried, "Show me a sign that Donny is with You. Let me know that he is all right!"

As I continued to dig in the garden, my hand shovel hit a rock. I picked at it with my garden tool, hoping to move it out of my way. Dusting the dirt off the rock, I found a gift from heaven, a perfect heart-shaped rock, light as a feather and flat as a pancake.

Running my fingers over the heart rock, I smiled and wiped my streaming tears. I knew that my beloved son, known for his big heart, was safe in the Lord's hands.

I have discovered seven more heart-shaped rocks in the garden I created in Donny's memory. My heavenly signs bring me comfort and remind me of Donny's happiness in eternity.

As I dig in the garden, now decorated with angels and eight heart-shaped rocks, I sense the Lord and Donny's comforting presence around me. I can imagine Donny grinning at my side, saying, "Not bad, Mom."

"...In the future, when your children ask you, 'What do these stones mean?'

tell them that the flow of the Jordan was cut off before the ark of the covenant of the Lord.... These stones are to be a memorial to the people of Israel forever."

JOSHUA 4:6,7

Margie Davis is happily married to Marvin who has been a strong support in her life, especially since the death of her son. Margie has three children and five grandchildren. She and Marvin live in Eugene, Oregon.

23

DELIVERED FROM DEATH'S DOOR
by Robert Edstrom

*A*fter I retired I spent the next twelve years volunteering as a chaplain for the Eastern Idaho Regional Medical Center in Idaho Falls. I witnessed God work in miraculous ways at the hospital. Many patients were healed and became born again during that time. Following are two testimonies of what I witnessed during my time at the medical center.

The first testimony is about a man I will call Joe who was admitted to the hospital with a lung problem. After leading him in the sinner's prayer to receive Christ as his Savior, I prayed for his healing.

When I entered his hospital room a few days later, he was despondent and staring at the ceiling.

"What's wrong, Joe?" I asked.

"The medical staff took a biopsy of the tumors in my lungs. The results showed that the cancer is fast growing," he stammered. "I only have a short time to live."

Not only was Joe devastated, but since I had prayed for his healing, I was too. I comforted him by saying, "We're still standing on the promises in God's Word that we had previously declared." We prayed together again, agreeing that God would answer our prayer.

When I called on him two days later, instead of being despondent there was now an excitement in his voice.

"What happened, Joe?" I asked.

"I just received the results of my new x-rays," he said. "The tumor is gone, and there isn't any sign of cancer! I'm healed and I'm going home!"

Joe was still doing well when I saw him five years later.

The second testimony is about Raymond Dunn who was hospitalized with a brain tumor that caused the left side of his body to be paralyzed. The first time I met him I introduced him to Jesus as Savior and then prayed for his healing. Then I asked if there was anything he could do now that he couldn't do before.

"I can move one finger on my left hand," he said.

A couple days later I visited Raymond again. He was beginning to move around and could get out of bed with some assistance. Shortly thereafter, he was walking the hospital halls with assistance, and soon after that he was walking without any assistance. The nurses called him their "miracle man."

Raymond continually told anyone who would listen how God healed him. He eagerly received encouragement from God's Word each time I visited him. His attitude also changed. He was no longer depressed but filled with life.

A month after being admitted to the hospital, Raymond wanted to be baptized in water. Since the chaplain supervisor and the hospital pool supervisor were not available, I contacted the nurse working at the pool and scheduled a time to baptize Raymond after regular pool hours.

The nurse on duty at the pool had admitted Raymond to the hospital. When she saw him, she was amazed at his recovery and gladly let us use the pool for the baptism.

Afterward, when we had changed into dry clothes, the nurse shared her excitement about Raymond's miraculous healing. I was talking to her about accepting the Lord when her boyfriend showed up. He had never belonged to a church. After he heard about Raymond's healing, both he and his girlfriend prayed the sinner's prayer. Only later did we discover that we were not supposed to use the pool for baptisms.

Raymond remained in the hospital for two more months. During that time, he inspired many patients and staff because of his positive attitude toward life and his continued healing.

> *how God anointed Jesus of Nazareth with the Holy Spirit and power, and how he went around doing good and healing all who were under the power of the devil, because God was with him.*

ACTS 10:38

Bob Edstrom is a field representative for the Full Gospel Business Men International in north Idaho. He and his wife, Jean, work with the area's local jails for the Chaplains Corp. Both are retired from their jobs but not from their work for the Lord. They live in Post Falls, Idaho.

24

MIRACLE SUPPLY IN
THE PHILIPPINES
by Jean Edstrom

My first husband, Steve, and I met while serving as missionaries in the Philippines. Bob had taken a missions concepts course for college credit and completed the course by spending a month in the Philippines. Not long after we met, we planned a September wedding and spent the month of October in Manila, Cebu City, and on the islands of Bohol and Negros.

Our contacts in Bohol, Cesar, and Esther Estacion, became lifelong friends. During our time in the Philippines, we traveled with them in their Ford Fiero to visit Christian believers throughout the island. We met Bible school students and taught Sunday school classes and were blessed to celebrate the seventh anniversary of the their church.

After returning home, I collected Bibles that my friends no longer used and mailed them to Esther so she could give them to the Bible school students. I also sent her Vacation Bible School material so she could translate the material for a VBS program she sponsored every April throughout the islands. I've done this for many years.

One year, all of my efforts to obtain VBS materials for Esther had failed. It was February and I didn't have a lot of time to send material to her before her upcoming classes in April. After praying about what to do, I felt led to talk to my associate pastor.

Pastor Dick listened to my plight and recommended that I contact Child Evangelism Fellowship (CEF) to find out what type of material they had. After I talked to the CEF Director, I learned that they had five different VBS kits; each included lessons and crafts for several age levels, pictures, music, and a missionary story.

I felt impressed to purchase the "Lost and Found" package. That evening I showed the kit to my church friends and took up an offering to cover airmail postage to the Philippines. The next morning I was thrilled to learn that the postage was only $20. I had imagined that both the materials and the postage would cost a lot more, so I included a check for the balance of the money that I had collected at church in the package.

When I got back from the post office that day, I had received a letter from Esther. She had started to work on the Vacation Bible School lessons and to my delight had chosen the theme "Lost and Found." However, she was having a hard time finding pictures to illustrate the stories and could not think of any crafts to go along with the lessons. I was excited because I had just mailed her everything that she was looking for.

The next letter from Esther told a more amazing story. Shortly after she mailed her first letter to me, her husband's father died. The family was obligated to travel to a distant island to be with Cesar's mother and family for a week of mourning that followed the funeral.

When they arrived home after the funeral, Esther stopped at the post office and found the VBS material she needed as well as a check that covered the extra expenses her family incurred because of the funeral. She was overwhelmed by God's timely supply of lesson materials and the money she needed.

A few years later, I received a letter from Esther informing me that she was very ill with kidney problems. She was unable to get out of bed and prepare for the upcoming Vacation Bible School that year. The only thing she knew to do was to commit both the work that God had called her to do and her healing to the Lord.

One afternoon my friend, Karen Tripp, came by to pray with me for my missionary friends. The Lord directed us to pray for Esther for the next hour. Some days later I received a letter from her that was written at the same time we were praying. She said that as she was lying in bed, the Lord had spoken to her and said, "You're being prayed for. Get on your knees and join in prayer for your healing."

Esther was obedient and soon sensed the warmth of God's healing touch. She was able to get up and go about her daily work. It took a couple of weeks to regain her normal strength, but she had been healed and was able to prepare and train the young people for another season of Vacation Bible School.

Over the years the Estacions have invited pastors, women, young people, and other groups to their church for conferences and camps. Regardless of the number of people who came for a conference, they would feed them three meals a day. Many times, however, they would run out of food before the end of the conference. Esther knew that if she went to the post office, she would find a check from me or from someone else to buy more food for the remainder of the conference. God has never failed her, though the timing may have been tight.

God promises that He will provide all of our needs by His riches in glory. (Phil. 4:19.) Both Esther and I have experienced great joy as we watched God work in supernatural ways to facilitate the spread of the Gospel in the Philippines through our prayers and obedience. Today, Esther and her team of teachers reach over 1,500 children a year during their April Vacation Bible School.

Look at the birds of the air; they do not sow or reap or store away in barns, and yet your heavenly Father feeds them. Are you not much more valuable than they?

MATTHEW 6:26

Jean Edstrom graduated from Prairie Institute of the Bible in Alberta, Canada. Not only did she serve a short mission in the Philippines with her late husband Steve, but was a missionary in China in the fifties and early sixties. Today, she and her husband, Bob, actively serve in the Chaplains Jail Ministry in Coeur d'Alene, Idaho. They have also been instrumental in developing two Full Gospel Business Men's Fellowships in northern Idaho.

25

FORGIVENESS BRINGS HEALING
by Chuck Dean

The room suddenly grew silent. Every eye was fixed on me as I stood beside the speaker's lectern. A deep, gnarly feeling in the pit of my stomach told me to run and hide. I stayed planted, not because I was a courageous man, but because God had told me to say what I had just said. I remained in place only through His strength.

After speaking the unspeakable before a group of over 200 Vietnam veterans, I read every emotion known to man on their faces. Some were shocked with unbelief; many wanted to take me outside, while others searched for reasons to leave the room.

In the course of teaching an anger management workshop, the Lord led me to tell this room full of warriors the unthinkable: I had forgiven a certain American actress for her gross misdeeds regarding the Vietnam War during the sixties and seventies, and I encouraged them to do the same.

After the initial assault on their sense of reality, they allowed me to continue without too much ruckus. Since I was also a Vietnam vet, they figured I deserved to be heard out before they strung me up.

I shared the story of God showing me the destructive personal consequences of harboring unforgiveness for someone who many consider to be a Vietnam-era betrayer of our country. I understood that as long as I couldn't forgive her, I was in relational bondage to her. God had spoken to my heart, "As long as you cannot forgive her, you'll have a spiritual relationship with her that doesn't please Me."

With this revelation I had quickly repented and forgiven her. "I forgave her because she was the last person on earth that I wanted to have a relationship with," I confessed to my fellow vets.

After asking the group for a show of hands of those who wanted to be free from this woman and what she represented to them, many hands shot into the air. As I prayed for these men's deliverance, the crash bars on the exit door banged open. I paused, looking up to see a big Marine in his wheelchair hurriedly leave the room.

Rob had been a hard-charging Marine in Vietnam until a machine-gun bullet caught him in the spine. He had been confined to a wheelchair for 20 years and accepted Christ as His Savior only a couple of weeks prior to the conference.

Seeing him flee the room, I suspected he was headed out to his car to get a gun. He told me later that the last thing he wanted to hear was a teaching about forgiving this person. Although he was a Christian now, there were still a lot of rough edges.

Thinking that Rob was disgusted with the idea of forgiving her, I shrugged off his quick departure and continued praying for the men who had raised their hands (most of the men in the room, by the way).

About an hour after the session, I was fellowshipping in the hallway with some of the men when we witnessed the surprise of our lives. Rob, who had not been out of his wheelchair for 20 years, walked in the door and marched straight into the cheering arms of the dozens of veterans who had just been freed from the soul bondage of unforgiveness.

When I asked Rob what happened, he said, "I decided to give in and prayed that God would help me to forgive that actress. When I said that prayer, my legs suddenly tingled with feeling. The sensation in my legs scared me so much that I went straight to the VA hospital to have them checked out. After probing around, they discovered that I had feeling in my legs. So I got up and walked out, leaving my wheelchair behind." Then, with obvious gratitude he added, "Not only am I free from her, but I'm free from my wheelchair, too!"

Hearing Rob give his personal testimony several times after that unforgettable day, I noticed that he never put much emphasis on his miraculous ability to walk again. In fact, every time I heard him testify about his Christian conversion, I had to remind him to testify about God healing his back and legs as well.

You see, to Rob, a man who knew the wretchedness of life from the inside out, just the simple fact that God wanted to save him from the pit of hell was enough of a miracle to last him a lifetime.

"When you stand praying, if you hold anything against anyone, forgive him, so that your Father in heaven may forgive you your sins."

MARK 11:25

Former Vietnam veteran Chuck Dean surrendered his life to the Lord Jesus in 1986. He wanted to see other Vietnam vets seek spiritual change by surrendering their lives to God. In 1987 he became the international director of Point Man International Ministries, a veterans support organization. Chuck is the author of several books, including "Nam Vet: Making Peace with Your Past."

26

THE EASTER BIRD
by Sheri Stone

"*I*'ve always wanted to be someone special. You know, like those people who talk to animals," my husband confided. "Do you remember the stories of children who were surrounded by birds? They talked to each other. That's what I would like—to be able to talk to birds."

Gene unashamedly divulged his secret to me as he intently watched the chattering flock of sparrows. Our walk to the lake that Easter morning had been prompted by his dislike of observing the orthodox Christian holiday. Although my husband had been raised with an agnostic point of view, he had begun to desire a closer relationship with our Savior. However, he struggled with letting go of his agnostic beliefs. The day before Easter he asked, "Why don't we have Easter service at the lake? Just you, me, and God."

Easter morning was spectacular. The sun's brilliance caused a shimmering glow on our surroundings, and its warm rays cloaked us as we walked down the road. Overcome with nostalgia, we began to share memories and dreams. We began to speak gentle words toward each other and were quickly united in our desire to touch the throne of God that morning.

Sensing the supernatural Presence of the Lord, we hushed to its authority. A flock of birds flew overhead, and Gene's secret was revealed. Any words spoken from my lips would have broken the tenderness of the moment. I nodded in silent agreement.

In quiet reverence we made our way to the lake and sat upon a rock jetty. Gene thumbed through my Bible and softly broke the quietude. "I want to find something in red ink to read," he whispered. "If I'm going to read anything, it must be a direct quote from Jesus. This book has a lot of red in it. I'll start here, in the book of John."

"John chapter one, verse one. 'In the beginning was the Word....'" He continued uninterrupted until the end of the chapter.

A slight rustling of nearby bushes caused Gene to pause. Noiselessly, a large flock of sparrows landed from their flight. They perched in the bushes and trees surrounding us, pivoting their tiny heads as if to listen to what was being said. Gene nodded his head to indicate their presence. I nodded in acknowledgment and motioned him to continue reading.

As the Scripture grew more profound, goose bumps covered my arms. The Lord spoke directly to Gene in the fourteenth chapter. "Do not let your hearts be troubled. Trust in God; trust also in me" (v. 1). He continued reading, "'...I am the way and the truth and the life. No one comes to the Father except through me'" (v. 6). I heard the rustling of bushes and looked up to watch the birds fly away.

That is, all but one who had positioned himself on the branch of a tree about fifteen feet away. He looked at Gene and cocked his head as if waiting to hear more of God's Word. Gene eyed the bird, "'If you really knew me, you would know my Father as well. From now on, you do know him and have seen him'" (v. 7).

The tiny sparrow moved closer; perhaps to hear better? From branch to branch, the fledgling drew near. Gene's words became slow and heavy, "'Peace I leave with you; my peace I give you....'" (v. 27).

The sparrow made his way to the rock upon which we sat. The bird and my husband looked at each other and began to commune. The little bird chirped and once again cocked its head in expectancy to hear more from the Word.

Gene had difficulty reading. All I could do was silently cry. When he finished John 15, the sparrow flew away. My husband looked at me, eyes moist with wonder, and said with a cracking voice, "God has poured His Spirit upon us. I'll never forget this day." We talked about our extraordinary visit and my husband's gratefulness to receive the fulfillment of his long-awaited desire.

"It's imperative that I continue reading until the red print ceases," he said. "...I tell you the truth, my Father will give you whatever you ask in my name...Ask and you will receive, and your joy will be complete" (John 16:23,24). Our feathered friend returned, first landing on a branch close by and then settling by Gene's side.

The two sat together as he read through John 17 and to the end of the red print. "Righteous Father, though the world does not know you, I know you, and they know that you have sent me. I have made you known to them, and will continue to make you known in order that the love you have for me may be in them and that I myself may be in them" (vv. 25,26). With that glorious word, the bird flew off, out over the lake.

Gene closed the Bible as we slipped off the rock and silently walked in awe to our house. We had witnessed an Easter miracle. Shortly after our early-morning encounter, Gene accepted Jesus as his Lord and Savior.

More than twenty years later, he enjoys sharing his life in Christ with others, especially his encounter with the Easter bird. Those who hear are captivated as he begins his story "I have always wanted to talk to birds...."

No one can come to me unless the Father who sent me draws him, and I will raise him at the last day.

JOHN 6:44

Sheri Stone is the director of the International Network of Christians in the Arts and the Songbird Christian Performing and Fine Arts Center, headquartered in Coeur d'Alene, Idaho. She is coauthor of this anthology as well as a screenwriter with her husband, Gene. The Stones have been married over forty years.

27

HIV POSITIVE NO MORE

by Linda Davies

I spent 25 years bound to drugs and alcohol. As a result of long-term heroin and methamphetamine use, I was hospitalized with a life-threatening blood infection. On the brink of death in 1998, my parents asked me to come home so they could give me the help I needed. Desperate, I agreed. On the way home to Moses Lake, Washington, I cried out, "Jesus, heal me!"

My mother later put me on an airplane to Fort Worth, Texas, where I enrolled in Teen Challenge, a one-year ministry program to assist people to overcome the bondage of addiction. After graduating, I remained on staff for another year while attending Bible school at Calvary Cathedral International.

On September 11, 2000, I received the devastating report that I was HIV positive. After hearing this stunning sentence from the doctor, a still, small voice inside of me said, "Don't fear, Linda. I'm going to heal you, and your testimony will be used to glorify Me."

I was not feeling well, and my health had already begun to deteriorate; so I returned to Spokane to be near my family and to seek help at the Healing Rooms.[1]

I narrowed the focus of my life to knowing God and His Word. I determined in my heart that regardless of how I physically felt or what the medical tests revealed, I would not question or doubt that my healing was on the way.

I read in the Bible that Jesus had already purchased my healing on the cross 2000 years ago when He took HIV and every other sickness and disease upon Himself. (Isa. 53:5.) I was determined to receive my healing from Him.

I also learned that if I remained in Jesus and His Words remained in me, I could ask Him anything, and He would give it to me. (John 15:7.) I saturated myself in the Word in order to plant the truths of the Bible in my heart. I looked up every healing story in the Bible, spoke healing Scriptures continually, listened to healing tapes, and took communion every night.

As I meditated on everything that God had done for me when His Son was crucified on the cross, the still, small voice reminded me that He was going to cleanse my HIV-infected blood.

I visited the Healing Rooms every Thursday. Their ministry team prayed for me and anointed me with oil. While I carried the infirmity of the HIV virus, Jesus continued to work on the inner issues that I had in order to bring my body, soul, and spirit into wholeness.

On my journey to healing, I read about the paralyzed man who was unable to find somebody to lower him into the pool of Bethesda so he would be healed. (John 5:2-8.) When Jesus asked him if he wanted to be well, of course he said, "Yes!"

When I read that Jesus told this man, ". . .Get up! Pick up your mat and walk," I realized that I had to do my part by getting up regardless of how hopeless my circumstances looked or how weak I physically felt. I knew that if I had the faith of a mustard seed (Luke 17:6), I could make this mountain of sickness move. I was fully persuaded that nothing was impossible for God, including healing me of the HIV virus.

I learned that faith comes by hearing the Word of Christ (Rom. 10:17), so I read my Bible continuously. I planted Scripture in my heart, watered it with prayer and praise, and then waited for a harvest of healing.

As the Word took root in my heart, my body began to feel better. Yet, I sensed an urgency to press in and seek God more diligently. I continually praised Him, and as I drew near to Him, He drew near to me.

One Thursday at the Healing Rooms they intensely prayed for me. As they prayed, I felt something happening in my belly. I began to groan and travail and dropped to the ground as if I was experiencing labor pains.

Something broke free in my spirit and brought a great release. After we finished praying, I felt emotionally, physically, and spiritually like a new person.

That same evening I attended a Full Gospel Business Men's conference in Coeur d'Alene, Idaho. During the meeting I met John Shepherd who was part of the ministry team. John had also been miraculously healed of HIV in 1997. I asked him to pray for me to be healed. I believed that when he laid his hands on me, I received my healing.

After the conference I went to see my doctor on March 3, 2001. He was amazed and commented on how healthy I looked. "I believe God healed me!" I testified.

He immediately ran tests to check my blood, and the results came back with the report that I had expected. The HIV was undetectable!

I thank Jesus for going to the cross and for bearing my sickness. Because of Him, I was cleansed and made whole.

> Then Jesus said to him, "Get up! Pick up your mat and walk."

At once the man was cured; he picked up his mat and walked....

JOHN 5:8,9

After being healed of HIV, Linda works at the Healing Rooms in Spokane, Washington. She enjoys sharing the testimony of her miraculous healing as well as telling others about God's love, grace, and mercy.

28

NOT A TEACHER!

by Ingrid Shelton

*W*hen I was in high school in the 1950s, my friends and I often discussed our future plans. I never wanted to teach. "A teacher?" I said. "Not me. Never!" My heart was set on becoming a nurse. I had already submitted my application for admission to the Regina General Hospital School of Nursing.

While contemplating my life as a nurse, the shrill ring of the hallway phone interrupted my dream. Rushing to answer the phone, the voice of the Director of Admissions of the Nursing School Department sent my heart into a spin.

"Miss Smith," she came right to the point. "We cannot accept you into our nursing program. Your health is far too precarious."

I gasped for breath as her words slowly sank in. I barely heard the explanation. The unexpected verdict sent me reeling to my room.

As a young teen, I had decided to become a nurse primarily because of the time I spent in hospitals. I could identify with patients, especially children. I could feel their pain, their insecurity, and their loneliness in being away from home. The thought that I could not physically handle the job never occurred to me. I felt that I could do anything I set my mind to. Even my high school teachers had realized that my poor health had not stopped me from achieving my goals.

They can't do this to me, my mind screamed as I flung myself on my bed, tears blinding my eyes. *How dare they stop me from becoming a nurse! Who decides what I should do with my life? Now what will I do?* I sobbed into the pillow.

Reaching for a tissue on the night table, I bumped my radio. On an impulse I turned the knob, hoping to drown the anguish inside of me. The harmonious voices of a hymn wafted into the room. The melody was unfamiliar, but the chorus soothed my wounded spirit. Over and over I heard the words, "God will take care of you." The rest of the words were lost to my troubled mind. A thought then came to me. *God!* I will ask Him what I should be.

God had been a stranger to me during my childhood. Only in the last two years had I realized that He really existed and that He was Lord of the universe. Yet, I was completely unaware that He was a personal God who would respond to prayer.

I eased to the floor and dropped to my knees. I wasn't sure about the correct procedure of addressing God. I didn't know any prayers, but I knew how to ask. "God," I began without introduction, "What do You want me to be?"

My prayer was finished, but I had no idea if and how God would answer. As soon as I had completed my request, I heard an audible voice, human in sound but different, say, "A teacher."

Stunned, I searched for someone to whom the voice could belong, even though I knew I was alone in my room. There was no one. I realized without a shadow of a doubt that I had heard God's voice. He had answered, but it wasn't the answer I wanted to hear.

Shaking and awestruck, I crawled back on my bed. *No, God! Not a teacher!* I screamed silently. *I'd rather wash dishes in a restaurant all my life. I would rather clean streets. Anything but a teacher!*

"A teacher." I heard that voice a second time, quietly yet audibly.

"All right, God," I cried softly with a mixture of apprehension and relief. "I'll be a teacher." With that decision made, my struggle ceased. A deep peace settled in my heart, yet at the same time I also knew that I would become a teacher not by choice, but by God's direction.

I kept my experience with God a secret. No one would understand, I reasoned. I believed people, including my family and friends, would think I had been dreaming or worse, I would be labeled mentally disturbed. I had never known anyone who heard the voice of God.

A few months later I enrolled in a teacher-training program. When I finally began to teach, I discovered that I enjoyed teaching more than I thought I would. As I searched the Bible, I found out that God always answers prayer when people call on Him, even though the answer may be different than expected. I finally understood that all I needed to do was to trust that He would show me what to do in any difficult situation for He promises to direct our paths.

After teaching for over forty years, I still tutor students. I love my job and would rather teach than do anything else in life. I am grateful to God for not only unmistakably guiding me to a profession that was best for me, but for also showing me that He answers prayer.

Many are the plans in a man's heart, but it is the Lord's purpose that prevails.

PROVERBS 19:21

Ingrid Shelton feels her greatest miracle was accepting God's love and grace through Jesus Christ. During the last forty years, she has taught all grades, from elementary students to adults. Ingrid and her husband, Philip, have one daughter.

29

TOUCHED BY THE GREAT PHYSICIAN
by Dr. Flo Ellers

By the age of three, my granddaughter, Rhonica's, developing legs had become bowed and her feet turned drastically inward. While running, she often fell as her bowed legs caused her to trip over her feet. Rhonica's condition troubled her parents, my husband, and me.

Although we hoped Rhonica would outgrow her problem legs, her aggravating predicament only worsened. Desperate to help her, my daughter took her to a doctor at the local clinic. X-rays indicated that both of her hips were turned inward.

"In order to turn her feet and legs outward, Rhonica will have to be put in a full body cast for several months," the doctor informed my daughter. "She'll have to wear shoes with an attached bar connecting them together to invert her pelvic bones."

Shortly after the trip to the doctor, I was babysitting Rhonica. I watched my granddaughter play outside and took notice when she started to run. Once again, because of her bowed legs, she tripped on her feet, fell forward, and hurt herself. The familiar tears flowed.

After witnessing the tumble, a righteous anger rose up inside of me. Furious that the devil was trying to steal my granddaughter's health, I stood up in boldness, marched over to her, and positioned her in front of me.

"Rhonica, stand right here." Unwilling to see my grandbaby suffer any longer, I put my hands on her hips and commanded, "I demand these hips to rotate *out* now in Jesus' name!"

Instantly, Rhonica's feet became completely and perfectly straight.

Today my grandchild is 20 years old and enjoys beautiful, long, straight legs. As her grandma I protectively advise her, "Don't wear anything too short, Rhonica. Your legs are too nice."

I tell you the truth, anyone who has faith in me will do what I have been doing. He will do even greater things than these, because I am going to the Father.

And I will do whatever you ask in my name, so that the Son may bring glory to the Father.

You may ask me for anything in my name, and I will do it.

JOHN 14:12-14

After graduating Bible college in 1982, Flo Ellers completed her doctorate in 2000. Through her itinerate ministry, Global Glory Ministries, she preaches the Gospel to the nations with signs, wonders, and miracles following.

30

PIERCING THE GLITTERING WEB
by Linda Nathan

The lone man walking in San Francisco's Haight-Ashbury District went unnoticed. If it had been known that he was praying for the residents in that neighborhood, he would have been unwanted. A new kind of awakening was happening in the sixties, one that was born on winds of rebellion, new philosophies, and drugs.

My husband, Richard, and I only had to walk out the front door of our Victorian apartment across from Golden Gate Park to experience this madcap community uprising. Although we had missed the Berkeley Free Speech revolt while in Europe, by 1965 the massive procession of hippies and anti-war protestors that came singing, arguing, and demonstrating under our windows more than compensated. Sometimes we wandered through the milling circus in a psychedelic high ourselves.

I thought Richard's family was romantic when we met in 1962. His father was a tough Marxist revolutionary who had known Mao Tse-tung before the 1949 Communist takeover in China, fought Mussolini in the Italian underground, and organized California's cannery workers. Now he provided for Richard and his two brothers in their dingy apartment above Ye Olde Anarchiste Bookstore.

Swept into the maelstrom that hit San Francisco in the sixties, we plunged into the new psychedelics and soon became fervent "evangelists" for them and the world of occult mysticism. To

Richard, drugs and paganism were an improvement over dreary atheism. To me, they promised freedom.

Strange spiritual visions and waking nightmares threatened to swamp my sanity in those early psychedelic seas, but they also stimulated my thirst for adventure. While all around us society was collapsing and being reborn, I walked a delicate balance through a surging inner tidal pool. For 14 years, we explored everything promising freedom: humanistic and psycho-spiritual therapies, Eastern religions, and "white" witchcraft. As "Lady Linda" in a New Age church, I gave psychic readings, reveled in "past life" visions, and "healed."

Surely, I thought, *we are on the cutting edge of a new revelation for the human race!*

By the early seventies, many of these changes were mutating into a widespread, interlocking, and rapidly expanding social and spiritual root system, known as the New Age movement. This movement was hurtling our nation away from its original basis in biblical morality toward blatant neo-paganism.

Belief in a personal godhead and salvation through self-knowledge was the movement's "glue." Experiencing this state was supposedly reached by manipulating "consciousness" through drugs, Eastern meditation, visualization, spiritualism, and psychic powers.

As we explored these dark regions, my psychedelic dream slowly turned into a ghastly nightmare. Somewhere in its deepest labyrinths, I began praying to Jesus Christ. At first I thought I was praying to Jesus when I prayed to the New Age "Ascended Master," and I prayed to the "highest good." God eventually honored my search for truth, although in a strange way.

Soon after a devastating miscarriage and cancer operation in 1976, I discovered that the cancer had returned and required an immediate hysterectomy. At age thirty-five, I found myself childless, in a disintegrating marriage, collapsing in graduate school from fruitless ambition, demon-ridden, and lost.

Everything was over for me, except for a strange sense of promise. But what could it be? All of freedom's promises had proven empty!

Days before my hysterectomy I visited a minister friend. He gave me a booklet and sent me into the chapel to read about a man whom Jesus Christ had miraculously healed of terminal cancer. In the stained glass light, I encountered words that changed my life forever: "It is a simple matter for Jesus to put His hand on the chaos that is cancer and bring order."

At that moment I felt that Jesus Christ radiantly met me, and I knew I was healed. He directed me to leave school, attend church, and prepare to have a baby. Repentance and salvation soon followed as He opened my eyes to my true condition as a wretched sinner under Satan's sway.

A second biopsy confirmed the healing, and the hysterectomy was canceled. My doctor had, in fact, been praying for me. After fourteen childless years, my son, Eric, was born a year later. I am still healed today.

My husband knew that a miracle had happened but still embraced the New Age beliefs. Nevertheless, he abandoned his goal of medical school to support me, and we attended church together. One afternoon while reading a tract, a sentence burned into his soul: "Satan tries to isolate a person to destroy him."

Satan! he thought. Only knowing the stereotypes about Christianity, he'd laughed at the devil's caricatures. But the idea of being isolated because of deceit was compelling. *What if there was a real spiritual being spinning a web of delusion over humanity?*

Suddenly, he saw a vision: The walls began shimmering with bright, gaudy images, like the childhood fun houses full of mirrors flashing distorted images. *All that glitters is not gold,* floated through his mind. He realized that the vision spoke of deception. Suddenly he understood that all of his New Age beliefs were glittering deceptions in a web of delusion that covered up the real condition of his life—bondage to sin. Sin was the other word that he had always laughed at.

A savior, he thought. *I need a savior. Jesus saves. So that's what Christianity is all about!* Right then he renounced the occult and asked Jesus Christ to save him.

In the years that followed, our lives have been rebuilt on the Bible, our marriage has been reborn, a wonderful child was given to us, and we have abundantly received the truth, purpose, freedom, and joy we had futilely sought as captives in the glittering web of New Age. And Richard, the former pagan atheist, earned a seminary degree.

All of this didn't just happen. My mother had faithfully prayed for us. And what about the man who walked the Haight-Ashbury District in the sixties? We met him nearly 25 years later. Today we are good friends and pray together for the lost.

> . . .*The prayer of a righteous man is powerful and effective.*
>
> JAMES 5:16

Linda Nathan and her husband, Richard, were miraculously delivered from New Age philosophies. They have been writing, speaking, and teaching about the New Age movement from a biblical viewpoint since 1980. They live near Mt. Baker, Washington, where Linda has her own writing, editing, and desktop publishing business.

31

OUT WITH THE OLD AND
IN WITH THE NEW
by Marcia Kyser-Karr

*M*y father was manic-depressive and attempted suicide many times throughout my childhood. He was the ultimate manipulator and was extremely skilled at controlling others. He often slept 20 hours a day, waking only when food was being served. Afterward, he would brag about the amount of food he was able to gorge.

My father's manipulative schemes and lies made it impossible for him to offer any love or guidance to me throughout my childhood. My mother was the pillar of our family and worked two jobs to keep everything going. Since she was never home, she only cooked from time to time. As a result, we ate a lot of tuna casserole with bread and butter.

When I was four, I received my first alarm clock. At that young age, I was responsible to get myself to kindergarten. Every morning I cooked my own hot cereal, packed a lunch, dressed myself, and arrived to school on time. Sometimes my clothes were dirty, worn inside out, or on backwards. I even wore the ill-fitting clothes of my older brother and sister. However, I always made it to school on time.

I began to hate people in the first grade. I hated everybody—teachers, parents, adults, boys, girls, "cops." I often turned in my homework with nothing written on the paper except the words, "I HATE YOU, I HATE YOU, I HATE YOU!" scribbled in the margins.

Dubbed the neighborhood terror, I didn't hesitate to beat up anybody. My classmates learned to never turn their backs on me. They either hated me or loved me. Although I was wild and vengeful, I could also be very generous. If I liked somebody, I would share with them the things I stole: dolls, trucks, candy, you name it.

One year I worked a lot of odd jobs in my neighborhood and saved $70 to buy a bicycle. Shortly after I bought the bike, somebody stole it. It was only then that I realized how wrong stealing was. Afterward, I hated everybody even more.

I thought my older sister was cool. When I was eleven, I often visited her at her home to smoke pot. By thirteen I was doing acid, THC, mescaline, and speed and had to work numerous jobs to support my growing drug habit.

After I was able to move out of my mother's house and get an apartment of my own, the hate I felt for people had somewhat diminished. I naturally gravitated toward rabble who were also shooting up, crashing in strange surroundings, and doing whatever they needed to do to make money for the next party.

As my life slowly began to unravel, I quit a good paying job as a waitress at O'Hare International Airport and took a minimum-wage job. The money I made was hardly worth the drive to work every day. In search of a better job, I found out that I could make good money by dancing.

At least it started out as dancing. In the beginning, I danced and mixed with customers. I collected the mixers from the drinks of men who bought me drinks and cashed them in at the end of my shift. It wasn't long, however, before offers to make some "real" money began to come in.

One night a friend told me about a concert she had heard about through a friend of a friend. My existence consisted of going to parties and getting high, so with the vague directions in hand, we set out to find the coveted jam session.

When we finally reached our destination, we thought we were lost. The building didn't look like a place where a typical rock concert would be held. Peeking inside, we saw hundreds of people and a stageful of instruments, so we went in and sat down.

Instead of hearing a rock group that night, we listened to an evangelist preach about God's forgiveness through Jesus Christ. I sat there for what seemed like hours. However, as this man talked, his words pierced my hardened heart. I tried to cover up the first few tears that trickled down my face by pretending that something was in my eye. But before I knew it, I was a bawling, broken mess.

My entire being was permeated with hate when I arrived at that divinely arranged meeting, but the unending tears dissolved the anger that had been buried deep within my heart for such a long time. That night I even prayed for my parents and forgave both of them. It was miraculous how the yoke of emotional pain lifted from off my back as God melted the anger and hatred that held me bound.

After the life-changing concert, I spent the next three days on my bathroom floor as my body convulsed from drug withdrawal. I thought I was going to die. Finally the shakes, chills, heaves, and sweats ended, and I was completely clean. My new life instantly emerged.

With a newfound vision for my future, I wanted to make something of myself, so I enrolled in the local community college. After my conversion to Christ, I quit my dancing job. I needed money for living expenses and knew that a minimum wage job would not be enough to meet my needs. I pondered on what kind of good paying job I could get without a high school diploma.

The temptation to return to my old life flashed through my thoughts, *Dancing will bring in more than enough money to pay the bills!* I quickly made an appointment to meet with the manager of a local club.

Traffic was heavy the day of the interview. As I was waiting for a light to turn green, I felt torn about returning to my old lifestyle. "God, if You don't want me to dance, give me a sign," I pleaded.

Suddenly, the driver of a blood red Cadillac in front of me put his car in reverse, stepped on the gas, and crashed into me! When the light turned green, the Cadillac drove away without a care. The driver never even got out of the car to see if I was all right. I tried to put my car in first gear but could not get the gears to engage. Finally relinquishing my will to God's will, I said, "Okay Lord, I won't dance anymore." I never did make it to the interview.

Of course, God doesn't make bad things happen to us. But the Bible says that all things work together for good. (Rom. 8:28.) That accident stopped me from going to the interview and sent a sign that changed the course of my life. A top-of-the-line luxury car reminded me that God gave me a precious gift, His Son Jesus. The blood red color of that Cadillac symbolized to me Jesus' blood that was shed for me on the cross.

It was now time for me to begin trusting that God would take care of me. Because I had started at such a young age to take care of myself, letting go and trusting God was a big step for me.

As I began to rely on the Lord, I was led to apply for a position at General Motors that same week. I was soon hired, and my boss was willing to work around my schedule at the community college. Later, I was accepted at one of the most competitive private schools in the country.

In less than three years, I graduated with honors while working full time. I even paid off $30,000 of school loans the year after I graduated. For the past 16 years, I have enjoyed a prosperous engineering career and have lived a happy life with my husband, Doug. God surely changes lives and takes good care of those who trust in Him.

Therefore, if anyone is in Christ, he is a new creation; the old has gone, the new has come.

2 CORINTHIANS 5:17

After kicking a ten-year drug habit, Marcia completed a mechanical engineering degree in record time. She graduated with honors and has enjoyed a successful engineering career for the past 16 years. Marcia and her husband, Doug, have been married for over 10 years and live in Portland, Oregon.

32

ALL BETTER, MOMMY

by Patty Mendez

My four children and I moved to eastern Washington from Chicago in the fall of 1998. We stayed with my sister and her four children until my husband joined us.

My sister's house has a main floor and a downstairs. The steps leading to the lower level have a decorative railing on one side and a partial wall on the other. Part of the stairwell is open to the lower level, which has a cement basement floor.

On September 18 my sister, the kids, and I were cleaning in different areas of the house. I was busily working downstairs in my nephew's room and paid little attention to the stairwell. My year-and-a-half old son, Jesse, came to the stairs to see where I was. He leaned over the partial wall and fell head first onto the cement floor.

I will never forget the sound of Jesse's head hitting that cement floor. It was a horrifying sound, like a watermelon bursting open. Immediately, I ran and scooped him up in my arms. I took him upstairs, applied ice to his head, and waited for him to calm down. Afterward, I took him outside for some fresh air.

When I looked into his eyes, I realized he was seriously hurt. His face was crazed, and I could also tell that he knew something was terribly wrong.

My sister and I rushed Jesse to the emergency room, where he was immediately examined. He was quickly admitted to the pediatric ICU. The golf ball size bump on his head did not appear very bad to me, and I felt he would be fine. As a new Christian, I knew I needed to pray and asked God to make sure Jesse would be okay.

The doctors wanted to take x-rays to determine the damage done to Jesse's skull. Because my son had to lie completely still for the x-rays, the technicians wanted to put him to sleep. I was not comfortable with giving him drugs, so I asked for a moment of quiet time to calm him myself.

In the darkness of the x-ray room, Jesse was strapped to the table. I asked God to keep him quiet so the technicians could take the pictures they needed. Immediately, a peace poured through me, and I had an assurance that Jesse would be fine. As I began to praise God, Jesse fell into a deep sleep. He did not move until the x-rays were successfully completed.

Dr. Demakas said the x-rays indicated a subdermal hematoma. Jesse's skull had been fractured, and he was bleeding internally. Because the location of the hematoma was of serious concern, Dr. Demakas transferred Jesse to the Children's Medical Center. Though the situation seemed to worsen by the moment, I continued to have a peace within me that Jesse's healing had already taken place. I knew my child would be fine.

Jesse stayed at the medical center overnight for observation. I was fully confident that his healing had already been completed, so I used the time to pray for the other children on the hospital floor. By morning Jesse's rapid recovery became obvious. He woke in good spirits, ready to play as a normal, active toddler. The bleeding had stopped; his hearty appetite returned. Because of his miraculous improvement, Jesse was released that day and scheduled for additional x-rays six days later.

When we arrived for the follow-up x-rays, I was again advised that he would need to be put to sleep because of his age. I said, "I don't want Jesse to be given drugs. Give me a minute with him." I prayed until he fell asleep. Once more, he slept until all of the x-rays were taken.

While I knew in my heart that my son was healed, the x-ray technician confirmed my feelings. "Why were these x-rays taken?" he repeatedly asked. They did not show any signs of head trauma! The doctors and technicians were unable to explain Jesse's miracle, but I knew Jesse was healed because of Jesus.

We live by faith, not by sight.

2 CORINTHIANS 5:7

Patty Mendez has been happily married for 16 years and is blessed with four wonderful children. Her family honors God with their lives and gives Him glory in all things.

33

THE GOD WHO HEALS
by Elroy (Al) Plue

In July of 1997, I was scheduled to see a VA doctor who wanted to perform exploratory surgery on me in order to pinpoint the numerous health problems I had been experiencing. The doctor I was scheduled to see had unexpectedly gone home, so instead, I saw the assistant surgeon.

After a casual conversation, he asked me, "Have you ever asked Jesus into your life?"

Startled by his question, I answered, "I've been looking for a church but haven't found one yet."

"You don't need a church to have a relationship with God," he replied.

"How do I do that?"

"Ask Him to come into your life, and He'll begin to direct your footsteps," he smiled.

That night I went into my bedroom, dropped to my knees, and said, "God, I hope You're listening because I sure want this to work. You see, I just can't live like this anymore."

I spent the next few hours reviewing my life and recalled how I had messed up my children's lives, my marriage of 28 years, and myself. "God, I need help. Please send me somebody. And God, if You can't help me, I don't want to wake up in the morning."

Two days later a business associate outlined the message of salvation to me and asked if I wanted to invite Jesus into my life. I responded, "Yes!" I became born again as I repented of my sins and accepted Jesus as my Savior.

One month later during a church service, I fainted. Although I tried to get up, I fainted three more times. Foaming at the mouth while being taken to the hospital by ambulance, I remember hearing the medic say, "I can't get a reading. Is he dead?"

Once at the hospital, the doctor immediately started an IV. He was bewildered as he looked at my test results. "You should be dead. You don't have enough electrolytes in your system to be alive!"

The next day a doctor was reading the x-rays that were taken at the VA hospital. He then sent me to see another doctor. Getting off the elevator, my heart sunk when I saw the sign on his door: *Byersdorf and Gates: Cancer Surgeons.*

When Dr. Byersdorf put my x-rays on the screen, he asked if I had seen the test results and if I knew what they meant.

"No," I said, wondering what news would follow.

He then explained that I had colon cancer and lymphoma cancer in my chest.

"What does that mean?"

"You need to be operated on immediately. Without surgery you have approximately ten days to live."

Shocked, I asked, "When do you want to operate?"

"First thing tomorrow morning," he said. "Go home and tell your family your situation." Then he added, "Because of your poor health, the odds of living through this surgery aren't good."

"What are my odds?" I wondered out loud.

"Less than 20 percent."

"Why have the operation then?" I asked.

"You'll die without surgery!" he said. "At least if you're operated on, you'll have some hope. Go home and try to muster up a
good attitude."

Taking his advice, I went to the home of my estranged wife. I
gave her the doctor's report and asked her to tell the kids. I then
went home to be alone. In my bedroom I began to talk to the Lord.

Being a new Christian, I had learned a few spiritual truths. I
knew from reading the Bible that when Jesus went to the cross, He
provided both salvation and healing for me, and all I had to do was
to ask Him to be healed.

I poured my heart out to God. "Lord, I know there's a time for
everyone to die. If my time is up, I'm prepared for that; but if I don't
have to go yet, I don't want to. I want to see my sons married and
to see grandkids." Thinking of my future I added, "I want to get my
house in order and give restitution to my family instead of the
heartache that I've caused them."

After talking with the Lord for a long time, I saw a vision of
a cloudy, soft blue sky. I could see the Lord's face as close as the
end of my nose. The vision began to fade, and I fell into a deep,
restful sleep.

At 3:30 in the morning, a bright light awakened me. A blue
haze surrounded the light and slowly moved from the corner
window toward me. I said, "God, is that You?"

The light penetrated my chest and warmth flowed though my
body. It rested awhile; and when it began to withdraw, an emotional
weight lifted off me. The light moved back to the corner where it
entered the room and seemed to hover there as if to say good-bye.

I laughed and cried. I knew God had touched me.

I fell asleep and awoke the next morning full of exuberant joy. Walking back and forth through my apartment, I repeated, "Thank You, Lord."

Checking into the hospital, the staff thought I was either in shock or just plain nuts. "What a great attitude you have," they said. Little did they know that the doctor would only have to do a "mop-up job." God had already done the real work.

Prior to the surgery, the doctor told me I would need a minimum of two weeks of round-the-clock monitoring in the intensive care unit and then three to five weeks of recovery.

When I awoke in intensive care, the nurse said, "If I didn't know better, I would say you never had surgery. All of your vital signs are normal!" The next afternoon I was moved out of the ICU unit. Every time the medical staff checked my vitals, they left my room shaking their heads.

Several doctors accompanied Dr. Byersdorf when he visited me. He described the lymphoma as an old cow pie that got too much sun. He said they scooped it up, did some trim work, and felt that they had gotten all of it. The colon cancer was also successfully removed.

Later, a nurse came in when I was up and said, "You shouldn't be out of bed!"

"But I have to go to the bathroom," I explained.

"You've got to be kidding," was all she could say.

My doctor frequently told me that I was the talk of his colleagues. Some said my recovery was a miracle; others said it was medically impossible.

The doctor soon asked, "Do you want to go home? We're not doing you any good here. All of your systems are normal, and you can rest at home." I was released from the hospital three days after surgery.

Initially, I was told that it would be at least two months before I could drive a car. I drove in four weeks. The doctor said it would be six months before I could return to work. I went back to work in two months.

Before starting a year of chemotherapy, I was told I would lose my hair, be sick, and lose weight. I had no sickness, kept all of my hair, and gained fifty pounds.

Five years after my surgery and after being told that I only had ten days to live, I am still going strong.

...for I am the Lord who heals you.

EXODUS 15:26

Al Plue has been an independent car dealer for 26 years. He gave his heart to Jesus in 1997 and testifies that it's never too late for anyone to turn to God. He is thankful for the physical health and spiritual life that God willingly gave to him.

34

THERE FROM THE BEGINNING
by Mary Suter

I was a Red Cross nurse working in Royal Air Force (RAF) hospitals during World War II. A young Canadian flying officer caught my eye, and I soon became one of the many British war brides.

Even though I was not a born-again Christian at the time, God's hand of protection surrounded me. Many times after I was transferred to a new RAF hospital, the hospital I just left was bombed.

Throughout the war I continually prayed, "Please, God, don't let the bombs fall on me!" He heard my prayers as time and again my life was spared. I didn't know anything about being led by the Holy Spirit, and many people told me that my timely escapes from disaster were due to my "woman's intuition."

One divine intervention particularly sticks out in my mind. At the beginning of the war, I was in training as a children's nurse in the East End of London. Because of the intense bombing, the nursery staff and children had been evacuated to the country.

One day the British Spitfires and German fighting planes were in heavy combat overhead. Inside the building we could clearly hear the raging engines as both sides battled for victory.

We were in the process of changing the diapers of the babies and pottying the older children before their afternoon naps when the air raid sirens went off. We grabbed the little ones off the potties and rushed down the well-worn stone steps of a very old spiral staircase. Under normal circumstances we would take one precarious step at a time, but on this occasion we flew down two and three steps trying to reach safety. I had two babies, one under each arm, and ran as fast as I could across the schoolyard to the air raid shelter.

The babies were screaming at the top of their lungs as the planes roared above us. As I ran to the shelter, I heard the shrapnel pinging around us, much too close for comfort. I swung the children in front of me as I burst through the shelter door just when I heard a bullet hit the ground behind me.

On the way out of the shelter after the raid, I noticed that the bullet had struck the ground where the children and I had been moments before. Only seconds separated my escape and the possibility of being shot in the back, possibly killing both the children and me.

This was just one of many miracles I experienced during the war. God took the time to answer my cries for help even though I rarely had time for Him.

After the war, Peter and I settled in Rocky Mountain House, a small horse-hitching town in Alberta, Canada. We later moved to the United States and by the early seventies were playing gentlemen ranchers on a 122-acre ranch in northern Idaho. We had horses, dogs, cats, and a cow. Peter owned a business in Spokane, Washington. I ran the farm, fed the horses, and mucked the barns. I loved every minute of it. By this time I had become a born-again Christian.

Early one Sunday morning, Peter, my son, Martin, and I saddled up the horses. I rode Snow, a spirited white quarter horse. Martin rode Rocket, another quarter horse just rearing to run. Rocket and Snow both wanted to take the lead and began to race.

If we had been in the Kentucky Derby, I would have won! However, Snow's bit slid up in her mouth, so I could not rein her to a stop as she belted down the narrow road. "Whoa," I yelled.

Martin was ahead of me. When he heard me yell, he turned to see my peril. He decided to race ahead of me, thinking that he would grab me off Snow as I passed by.

Unfortunately, Snow saw the barn and made an immediate about face to race home. Needless to say, I didn't stop. I flew off of the horse like a jet-propelled rocket and bounced on the dusty road before tumbling to a stop. Unfortunately, as I fell to the ground, Snow's hoof hit me in the head. I don't remember much after I fell except that my left leg was thrown across my chest and the pain was unbearable.

Friends who had witnessed the accident quickly called an ambulance. When the paramedics arrived at the scene, they gave me a painkiller. After I reached the hospital, the doctors would not give me anything more for the excruciating pain.

Lying in my solitary corner of the emergency room, I looked out the window and began to bargain with God. "If You will please take away the pain, I will...." *What will I do?* I thought. *I'll have to give up the one thing that I enjoy the most. Whoa! What am I doing? Well, I really enjoy cocktails....*

I thought hard about the sacrifice I would have to make. As the pain grew in intensity, I cried, "God, I'll give up hard liquor." Peter and I enjoyed martinis every evening before dinner, so giving up my daily cocktail was quite a sacrifice.

God does not cause pain. His love for us is unfathomable, and He wants us to be well. I believe that submitting to His will for me allowed Him to move in my life and brought about a healing from the pain—immediately it was gone! I felt wonderful! And from that day to this, I have never had another drink.

A few months later the doctors informed me that I had two fractured discs and wanted to operate immediately. Having heard horror stories about back surgeries, I went home instead. My doctor continued to insist on surgery, and eventually I relented. The surgery went well, and I left the hospital in a steel brace from my shoulder blades down to my thighs. I could only bend my knees.

To fuse the vertebrae together, the doctor removed bone from my hip. I was again in a lot of pain and lived on painkillers. My hip and back hurt from the surgery and the steel brace cut into my body. Peter often held me as I cried in misery.

Every day my wonderful husband washed my back, rubbed it with alcohol and baby powder, and redid my brace. The days soon turned into weeks and months. Then it hit me! If God could heal me of the pain I had experienced earlier, He could heal my fractured discs. Ephesians 6:11-17 took its rightful place in my life. I put on the whole armor of God and went into battle.

I said to Peter, "Please find me someone who can pray for my healing."

Peter invited a young minister and one of the elders in his church to come to our home and pray for me. When they laid hands on my back, a warm, soft feeling enveloped me from the top of my head to the tip of my toes.

The pain and discomfort of the surgery left me that day and never returned. When the time for a scheduled appointment with my doctor drew near, I thought that I should have a heart to heart talk with God. Even though I was scheduled to wear the steel brace for six months, I prayed that the doctor would put me in a light brace.

Peter took me in for x-rays, and we waited in the doctor's office as he reviewed the film. He looked at the x-rays for a long time before putting them down. "I've never seen such a quick healing. I think I'll put you in a light brace," he said.

You can imagine the noise that resounded from that office. It wasn't long before I was out of that brace. I experienced none of the predicted aftermath that most people suffer. Isn't God wonderful? He knows what we need and when we are ready to receive it. I have now been healed for over thirty years.

...The reason the Son of God appeared was to destroy the devil's works.

1 JOHN 3:8

Mary Suter met her husband, Peter, during World War II. During the war, she survived many bombings and air raids. When the war finally ended, the Suter family moved to Canada, Peter's native country. In 1961 they left Canada to reside in the United States. Peter passed away in 2000. Mary has settled into her little condominium with her poodle, Elizabeth. She commits much time daily to prayer and reading the Bible.

35

GOD'S PLAN FOR PROVISION

by Pastor Mike Walker

My wife, Jane, and I had not been married long when we received a call from my sister's pastor to quickly come to St. Joseph's Hospital in Lewiston, Idaho. My sister, Jean, had been in a motorcycle accident and was not expected to live. We immediately rushed to the hospital.

In addition to a badly broken and bruised body, Jean's lungs had collapsed. After emergency surgery, she was hooked up to all sorts of life-support machines. The nurses turned her comatose body every hour to keep her circulation flowing properly. Only two family members at a time were allowed to visit her in the intensive care unit.

During one fifteen-minute interval, I went in to see Jean with her pastor. While we were there, she stopped breathing and her heart monitor flatlined. She was dead. The ICU staff immediately rushed into the room and feverishly, but unsuccessfully, tried to revive her. Pastor Tucker grabbed her foot and commanded, "In the name of Jesus, I speak life!"

Jean revived the moment those words were spoken. She later testified that her spirit hovered in the room after she died and then reentered her body through her feet when Pastor Tucker prayed. My wife and I both accepted Jesus as our Lord that day!

Since that time, we faithfully served God and eventually became pastors of Faith Tabernacle in Post Falls, Idaho.

Early in our ministry, the Lord spoke to us about purchasing property to build a church. At that time we only had thirty-five people in our congregation, including the children. We signed a contract for five acres of land and obtained a building permit. We started the project with $300 and an obedient heart to follow the Lord.

A lumber mill donated enough material to build the forms for the concrete footings and a cement company donated the steel rebar needed for the footings. After praying, I felt led to ask another company to donate the plywood we needed, and they willingly gave us thirty-five sheets.

We now had the materials we needed to build the foundation but no money to purchase the cement. After several weeks had passed, we were not able to raise any of the finances for the building. I knew that storing the plywood in the weather would eventually deteriorate the wood.

One afternoon I desperately prayed, "Lord, You told us to build, and You said You would supply. We're becoming the laughing stock of the town. We've started what You've told us to do, but we can't continue!"

In my heart I heard the Lord clearly say, "Get to work!"

"What?" I said. "We can't do anything. We don't have any money!"

The Lord responded, "You don't need money until you've done everything you can possibly do; then I will supply."

As that word stuck deep in my spirit, I received a revelation. *God will supply all of our needs since this need is based on His Word.*

I called some of the men from the church, and we made the forms for the foundation. On the second day of work as the men were beginning to leave, a man who was new to the church drove into the parking lot, jumped out of his truck, and tucked a $500 check in my shirt pocket. In a gruff voice he said, "Here!" then got back into his vehicle and sped away.

We poured concrete the next day. The remainder of the building was built the same way as God provided our every need.

For the first three years that Jane and I pioneered Faith Tabernacle, I taught adult Sunday school, preached both Sunday morning and evening, Tuesday evening, and every other Thursday night. I also had a physically demanding full-time job stacking wood in a lumber mill. In addition, Jane and I were also raising three young sons.

I reached a point where I realized that I had to boldly step out in faith and trust God to financially supply the needs of my family. When I looked at the finances of our church, I realized that I was supplying more than a third of the church's tithe. I often wondered how God would work out our finances.

One day after I had finished running the line at the lumber mill, I heard the Holy Spirit whisper in my heart, "Give your notice."

Boy did that scare me! I grabbed my Bible and headed to the break room. As I pulled up my chair to the round laminated table, I opened my Bible and it fell open to Haggai 1:8 KJV, "Go up to the mountain, and bring wood, and build the house; and I will take pleasure in it, and I will be glorified, saith the Lord."

On June 1, I gave a thirty-day notice, and by mid-July, I was ministering in Nigeria. Someone had paid for my ticket. I returned from Africa excited about what the Lord had done during my three-week stay in a spiritually bound land, and my hopes were high as I knew in my heart that He would continue to provide my every need.

However, I soon sold my fishing boat, my pickup, and many other "things" to meet the needs of my family. I tried my best to help the Lord to provide for us but soon ran out of options. I couldn't bring myself to sell Jane's things. We soon ran out of everything, including food. We didn't even have a bottle of ketchup. Although we were broke, we never told anyone about our condition.

One Saturday, we fed the boys the last of our food and put them to bed. Jane went into the bedroom and cried. I went to the living room to pray. Angry with God I yelled, "What's happening, Lord? We've always been faithful tithers."

A fervent, effectual prayer began to roll out of my spirit. I shouted, "Lord, I've obeyed Your Word. Don't You have an obligation to keep Your end of the deal?"

When I got quiet enough to listen, I heard Him say, "Seek first the kingdom of God."

"And what do You think we're doing? Our entire life is devoted to further Your kingdom!"

Again I heard, "Seek first the kingdom of God and My righteousness and all these things will be added unto you!"

This time I understood what He was saying. God was not going to move because we had a need. He was going to move because He is faithful to His Word. He said that if I sought His kingdom first, then all of my needs would be met. Since ministry was first in our lives, I *knew* God would come through for us.

That Sunday morning, we expected to find our answer in the offering plate. It wasn't. However, someone placed a sack in our car that contained potholders and pumpkin pie filling. Since pumpkin pie filling is food, I began to shout and praise the Lord. Jane looked at me as though I had lost my mind.

We dropped by Jane's parents and ate dinner that day. In my spirit, I heard the sound of abundance. At the Sunday evening service we did not receive any money in the offering; however, someone put four bags of groceries in our car. Later that week we received a $300 check from a man we met in another city. We were able to pay some bills.

Not knowing of our condition, the pastor of a church in Lewiston was praying for my family, and the Lord impressed him to take up a food offering for us during his midweek church service. A member of his congregation was driving to Post Falls in two days and would deliver the food to our church.

During our Thursday Bible study, we thought the answer to our financial need would come in the offering. It did not, but we found four more sacks of food in our car. One day we left our home for a short time and returned to find four bags of groceries on our doorstep. The next day the food from Lewiston arrived. For two weeks food was continually given to us until our pantry was so full that we had to add more shelves. We even gave food to other people who were in need. We have never lacked since that time!

Two years later I was in Nigeria teaching one hundred Nigerian pastors. Some of these men had many churches under them. I began to notice that their children were not being taught about the Lord. Because many of the children worked to support the family, few of them attended any of their church's programs. I felt that I must address this issue with the pastors.

As I finished my lecture, the room grew cold with silence, and I opened the floor for questions. The eldest minister came forward, took one of the microphones, and challenged me in front of the other pastors.

"This is easy for you to say. Your government helps you with welfare. We have to believe God for everything. Even our food has to be prayed in."

I finally understood the reason why my faith was challenged when I first stepped out in faith. As I shared how my wife and I also had to trust God for the food, the pastors wept uncontrollably as they realized that even American preachers face trials in the same way that they do.

I shared God's provisional answer to their needs. As they obediently follow after God and His Word, He will supply all of their needs. They only need to expect His provision for He is the great Provider!

Blessed be God, even the Father of our Lord Jesus Christ, the Father of mercies, and the God of all comfort,

who comforts us in all our tribulation, that we may be able to comfort those who are in any trouble....

2 CORINTHIANS 1:3,4

Mike Walker pastors Faith Tabernacle in Post Falls, Idaho. He and his wife, Jane, teach their congregation to expect miracles. Mike and Jane often travel to Nigeria to share their faith with Christians living in the midst of a predominantly Muslim society.

36

THE VOICE OF THE GOOD SHEPHERD
by Pakeerasin Horobiowski

Late one afternoon in the early part of 1995, my one-year-old daughter, Angela, and I were playing in front of our house in Pattaya City, Thailand. I had some household chores to tend to so I asked Joe, my thirteen-year-old neighbor, to keep an eye on Angela for a short time. I went into the kitchen and began to prepare rice for dinner. As I was working, I heard an audible voice say, "Find Angela."

Sensing an urgency I ran out to the terrace but only found Joe. "Where is Angela?" I asked.

"I don't know where she is," Joe said. "She was here just a minute ago!"

I panicked. As I walked around the side of the house, the audible voice commanded, "Go to the pool."

The pool was only 10 meters away. As I ran across the street, I saw people sitting on a bench near the pool.

"Have any of you seen Angela?" I shouted.

"No, we haven't seen her," they assured me.

Not wanting to waste any time, I turned back to continue my search at the house. I only took a few steps when I heard the firm, audible voice repeat, "Go to the pool!"

I ran past the people and saw Angela submerged face down in the water.

Joe's mom was near the pool. When she heard my cry, she jumped up, dove into the water, and dragged Angela out of the pool.

"Help! Help me!" I cried as Joe's mom laid Angela's limp and unconscious body on the concrete. Her skin had turned a greenish purple color, her fingernails were purple, and her stomach was greatly enlarged.

Billy and Gary, two fishermen who lived in a nearby house, heard my cries for help and came running. They performed CPR on Angela and covered her tiny body with their shirts to warm her.

As they worked on her, I fervently prayed at her side. Not able to put my prayer into words, I pled for Angela's life in an unknown tongue. The people who had gathered at the pool thought I had lost my mind, as my intercession could not be understood.

Within five minutes, Angela began to vomit.

As the ambulance pulled up, my husband, Leo, arrived home from work. He noticed the commotion and started to walk to the pool to see what happened. When he saw Angela, he ran to our sides. As Leo held me, I continued to pray in other tongues.

The ambulance sped our daughter to the hospital, where the doctors immediately ordered chest x-rays and other tests to determine if there was any damage to her brain. Miraculously, all of the tests indicated that she did not have any brain damage, and they couldn't find any water in her lungs.

We weren't satisfied with the hospital care and wanted to be sure that Angela was fine. We, therefore, took her to a second hospital where they reran the tests. Again, all of the tests came back negative! She was kept in the hospital overnight for observation and released the next morning.

Angela was back to normal the next day. The near drowning seemed like a dream. Her miraculous recovery was a testimony to the neighbors who witnessed the incident as they realized that God had saved and preserved her life.

My sheep listen to my voice; I know them, and they follow me.

I give them eternal life, and they shall never perish; no one can snatch them out of my hand.

JOHN 10:27,28

Pakeerasin (Pum) Horobiowski was born in Thailand and came to the United States with her husband, Leo, in 1997. She graduated with honors from Destiny Ministry Training Center in Spokane, Washington, in 1999. Pum, Leo, and their nine-year-old daughter, Angela, hope to eventually return to their homeland.

37

GOD SAVED MY MARRIAGE

by Kathy Gilmore

$\mathcal{T}$he moment I saw Paul I knew he would one day be my husband. Although not exactly love at first sight, I never doubted the calm sense of certainty and commitment God gave me from the beginning. On our second date, a bombshell shattered my image of romance in paradise. While we were hiking, Paul pointed to some hikers and said, "You see those people? They're gay, and so am I."

Millions of questions flooded my mind after he spoke. Faced with making a decision to either cement or destroy our relationship, I asked myself, *What do I really believe?*

I was raised as a Christian, but my Christian faith seldom impacted my feelings or actions. Always the straight kid in our family, I painted an outward appearance of innocence but hid the dirty side of my life. Anger, fear, self-pity, and selfishness drove a convincing performance.

Several years after a homosexual encounter with a fifth-grade girlfriend, my attention shifted to boys. Some form of physical contact was present in all of my relationships, yet physical stimulation could not satisfy my desire for love and intimacy. While constantly seeking the reassurance that I was loved, I found that the more I sought to be loved, the less I was able to give it.

Jumping from one boyfriend to another, I concluded that I would never love anyone. Selfish and unfaithful, I was driven to find someone who could make me feel loved and satisfied.

Overcome with loneliness, I asked myself, *What do I really believe?*

Although I knew that Jesus died for the sins of the world, I didn't understand that He died for the sins I was ashamed of. I didn't realize that His blood covers the sexual exploration I had experienced with a female friend, the promiscuity, my selfish desire to be loved, and all of the ugly things in my life. Once I understood that Jesus died for me, a hopeless sinner, I accepted Him as the Lord of my life. Finally my beliefs and my lifestyle were united.

I was unsure if people were born homosexual or grew into it. I did know, however, that homosexuality was a sin. I knew the Scripture called all wrongdoing sin and that all sin had the same penalty and solution.

When Paul shared his challenge with homosexuality with me, I had to admit that his struggle was no different from mine with sin. There wasn't any doubt in my mind that Paul was seeking God with all of his heart, so we eventually married.

After five years of marriage, I was pregnant with our second child when Paul announced that he wanted a divorce. He left us and moved in with another man. Before leaving, he admitted that his sexual partners were so numerous that he lost count and confessed that his longest span of faithfulness during our marriage was eight months. At that time, AIDS dominated the media headlines. The news of his promiscuity was devastating.

Paul, however, returned home shortly after he left. He came to the conclusion that his children's needs were more important than satisfying his selfish desires for sex, freedom, and pleasure.

Noble as his motives were, it was not much in which to rebuild our marriage.

The man I married no longer existed. Paul had become a complete stranger. He had lied, cheated, and betrayed our sexual intimacy. Not only had the foundation of our trust been violated, he risked the health of our children and me as well.

I tried to forgive him and put the past behind me, yet forgiveness alone was not enough to restore our relationship. Paul claimed that he was no longer physically active in the homosexual lifestyle, but he continued in patterns of emotional isolation and self-sufficiency. Treating me more like an object than a person, Paul acted as if I was the enemy of his desires and the reminder of his failings.

In his search for independence and a "manly image," we built a log house and lived for four and a half years without electricity and sometimes without running water. Now raising five children, we homeschooled them by kerosene lantern.

Another bombshell soon hit the fabric of our lives. Paul and two of our children were diagnosed with Hepatitis B, a disease commonly found in the homosexual community. Paul and one of the children's conditions had already progressed to a chronic state. According to doctors the disease was untreatable, incurable, and would eventually be fatal. Feeling betrayed and abandoned by God, I was unable to bear the news.

The calm assurance I had when I first met Paul stood in stark contrast with the pain, rejection, and loneliness that I now felt. Every ounce of faith, hope, and love that I once had was shredded.

I cried out, "God! You don't understand! My child is innocent!"

In my heart I heard Him answer, "I understand."

"But my child will die because of his father's sin!"

"My Child died for yours."

"But he doesn't deserve to die!" I cried.

"Neither did My Son."

In anger and despair I told God "I'm through! I can't go on. Even if You're real, I don't want to follow You anymore. I can't and won't believe in You when it hurts like this."

As my pain continued to mount, I wanted to destroy my relationship with God, yet He spoke life into our relationship and kept it going. Grieving over the impact of sin in our lives, I wept, fasted, and prayed for the next four months.

One night after my husband returned from a Promise Keepers[1] weekend, he renounced his spiritual commitment to sexual gratification, pride, and misguided feelings of immunity from judgment of his sin. An intense time of prayer, repentance, and inner cleansing lasted for four hours that night and extended throughout the next two weeks.

I saw an immediate change in Paul. His resentment toward family members evaporated. He stopped controlling me and was no longer compelled to visit places where he was sexually tempted. He quit hiding where he spent his money and even changed his eating habits. He literally looked and acted like a new person.

The fabric of our unraveled lives became individual threads. Some of the threads were remnants of Paul's old way of thinking. As those threads became visible, the breath of God's Word easily blew them away. Threads of character, integrity, honesty, humility, and patience, which for so long had been invisible, had now become vibrant and strong, weaving a new fabric for our family.

In 1998 we participated in an experimental study for a new Hepatitis treatment for children. The most the doctors could offer was a remission of the disease, delaying the effects of the disease, and prolonging their life expectancy.

After a year in the program, test results indicated the disease was virtually cured. The virus was undetectable and was no longer able to reproduce. Our children's antibodies were actively destroying new virus cells. It was the first case in that clinic to achieve such results.

In February of 2004, Paul and I will celebrate our twenty-third wedding anniversary. He is a new man and is completely free from homosexuality. I am also a new person because I learned to allow God's love to flow through me.

If my people, who are called by my name, will humble themselves and pray and seek my face and turn from their wicked ways, then will I hear from heaven and will forgive their sin and heal their land.

2 CHRONICLES 7:14

Kathy Gilmore and her husband, Paul, are co-directors of Metanoia Ministries, a personal outreach Web ministry encouraging a Christian lifestyle centered on repentance.

38

LIVER TRANSPLANT CANCELLED
by Pastor Gene Ross

$\mathcal{O}$ver the 40 years that I have served as a pastor, I have faced several health crises, but in March of 1993 I encountered the biggest challenge of my life.

I was living in St. John, Washington, when I awoke one morning feeling sick. I made an appointment with my doctor, but after an examination, he was unable to offer a diagnosis. For several months my health continued to fail. Finally, I was transferred to a specialist in Spokane, Washington.

In December, I visited the University of Washington Medical Center in Seattle for thorough medical testing. After the test results were analyzed, Dr. Carithers, a liver surgeon, explained the diagnosis to me.

"Gene, you're suffering from a disease called Primary Sclerosing Cholangitis. The disease is destroying your liver bile ducts," he said. "In your present health, you have about a year to live. You must receive a liver transplant."

I returned to St. John and continued to pastor at Christian Life Assembly of God. I lost 35 pounds, and fatigue plagued me daily. Although I continued to minister at the Sunday services, I had to rest during the week to regain my strength.

Eventually, my family and I agreed that a liver transplant was necessary and my name was placed on a waiting list. The cost of the operation was not covered by my health insurance. A network of family and friends began to raise $250,000 to cover the operation. The appeal for financial help stretched across the country and into several nations around the world. Donations totaling $176,000 were sent to an organ transplant fund in Nashville, Tennessee.

My strong faith and that of others helped to sustain me during these dark days. On one occasion my entire congregation stood in the front of the church to pray for me. Countless friends and fellow pastors supported me in prayer and encouragement. I received cards, letters, and prayer support from people representing numerous denominations across the globe coming together in unity on my behalf.

Although I had no inkling of what the final outcome of my illness would be, I enjoyed complete peace that surpasses all understanding. Knowing that God has ordained my steps, I rested in the confidence that my life was in His loving hands. Early in 1994 my appetite began to return and my energy level increased. I had been traveling back and forth from St. John to Spokane throughout this time for blood tests. In May, the tests revealed a change for the better. Dr. Grossman, a specialist in Spokane, gave me the initial good news. "You know, this is a miracle. This just does not happen with this disease."

I smiled and said, "I know that hundreds, perhaps thousands of people have been praying for me."

Dr. Grossman replied, "I've been praying for you, too."

When the doctors in Seattle received the latest news about my condition, they were not as optimistic. I traveled again to Seattle for additional tests. After examining the results, Dr. Carithers repeated the good news. "I would never recommend a transplant for you in this condition. You're too healthy!"

In September 1994, I was removed from the liver transplant list. The money that had been raised for my no-longer-needed transplant was dedicated to transplant-related needs through a national organ transplant foundation. In December, two days before Christmas, lab tests revealed that my blood was completely normal. Since that time, I have not needed any medication. My energy level is back to normal, and I am thankful to be alive.

Praise the Lord, O my soul, and forget not all his benefits—who forgives all your sins and heals all your diseases.

Psalm 103:2,3

Pastor Gene Ross is currently on staff at his son's church, North Seattle Christian Fellowship in Seattle, Washington. He and his wife, Barbara, work with "Primetimers," a seniors' group.

39

GOD'S POWER TO HEAL
by Evangelist Eric Cowley

*I*n 1984 and 1985 I held crusades and church meetings throughout the Philippines. After preaching at a crusade meeting one afternoon in Buyuan, I asked my missionary friend to speak in my place that evening. "Chester," I said, "please speak for me tonight. But when you have finished preaching, leave some time for me to pray for the sick."

After Chester had ministered the Word, he called me up to the platform. Prompted by the Holy Spirit, I asked people with back problems to come forward. Out of the 400 people who were crammed into the building, ten responded to my invitation.

After praying for these people, I asked each of them to do something they could not do before. Afterward, all ten testified to being completely healed. Faith saturated the room.

A woman edged toward the platform and asked me to pray so she would be healed of the large egg-sized goiter that protruded from her neck. Although I had not asked for people with goiters to come forward, her faith had been stirred after witnessing the healings of back problems.

Chester and I both laid hands on her neck at the same time. At first nothing happened. I looked at Chester and said, "Watch!"

The Lord impressed me to form my hand like a pistol. I put my pointer finger on her goiter and commanded, "Shrivel and die, in Jesus' name." The goiter instantly disappeared!

Another woman with a goiter came forward. When I looked at her, I saw into the spirit realm and could see the cause of her illness.

"A lot of what we see in the natural world is the manifestation of something in the spiritual realm," I said to Chester.

In the spirit I saw a black creature about 12 to 16 inches long wrapping its sharp, clawed hands around the woman's neck as if trying to strangle her. I knocked the creature from off her neck with my hand but saw that it buried its face in the back of her neck. I commanded, "Get off of her, in Jesus' name."

As she walked back to her seat, she felt her neck to see if the goiter was still there. "I'm healed! I'm healed!" she screamed. The goiter had completely disappeared.

The next woman who came forward had a monstrous goiter the size of a small cantaloupe on the left side of her neck. She wore a red scarf in an attempt to hide it. When I asked her to take off the scarf, she slowly removed it, obviously embarrassed about her unsightly deformity.

The Lord impressed me to lay my hand on her shoulder. I said, "Woman, God touches you."

I knew that as I released my faith, God would heal her. Within minutes, the goiter was completely gone. The woman kept putting her hand on her neck to see if the goiter had returned. I instructed her to keep her hand down and told her not to be afraid that she would lose her healing. As everyone in the auditorium witnessed her healing, God's love and compassion penetrated the auditorium.

A five-year-old boy who had been born blind was then brought to the platform. The iris of his eye was a darker white than the rest of his eye. The Lord prompted me to lay my hand on his eyes and say, "Blind spirit, come out of his eyes, in Jesus' name!"

We watched intently. Within five minutes the irises of his eyes turned from pale blue to brown. The child's father was next to him as the interpreter asked, "What can you see?"

"I can see light!" the little boy answered. His eyes improved by the second.

All of the people in attendance at the Buyuan crusade were eyewitnesses to the many wondrous miracles that God performed as His name was lifted up.

...And the power of the Lord was present for him to heal the sick.

LUKE 5:17

Eric Cowley is the founder and president of WorldWide Harvest, an evangelistic outreach ministry with offices in the United States, England, and Canada. He has held crusades in over forty nations around the world. Eric and his wife, Gillian, live in North Bend, Washington, with their daughter, Jessica.

40

WALKING IN GOD'S LOVE
by Robert Yates, Jr.

*W*hen I'm taken to the south cellblock cluster to shower, I am normally able to do what I need to do without any disturbances. This day was different. The inmates from this cellblock cluster were locked in their cells; and while I was being uncuffed and unshackled, an inmate shouted, "Are you Robert Yates, the 'whore killer'?"

The other inmates quickly confirmed that his suspicions were correct. For the duration of my shower, he yelled profanities at me and pounded uncontrollably on his cell door. His wild actions were so loud that the control booth officer entered the cluster twice to try to quiet him.

As I listened to his cursing and hateful words, my flesh began to rise up in anger. I wanted to say, "Grow up. Who made you righteous," but I didn't. Instead, the Holy Spirit led me to pray for him. I realized that he was trying to take his hurt and anger out on me. I asked God to free him from his pain and torment. Then I strongly rebuked Satan.

Shortly before I finished showering, a guard entered the cluster to check on the inmate's hands to see if he had broken them when he pounded on the door. The guard told the inmate that he would try to get a nurse to look at his hands and then left.

When I stepped out of the shower, the inmate continued to taunt me and demanded that I face him.

"Let me look in your eyes," he snarled. "I want to see the evil that possesses you."

"You won't find evil in me," I assured him as I walked up to his cell. "You'll only find love." As he looked me in the face, I added, "Don't worry about what you said earlier. It's already forgotten. I know you didn't really mean it anyway."

"Your reaction to me is pretty common. I get angry responses from people because of the crimes I committed before Jesus came into my life," I continued.

I then told him about my love for God and that I was a father of five children.

"Why did you murder all of those women?" he asked.

"I wish I could understand that myself," I answered. Then looking at his hands I asked, "Are your hands all right?"

"I think I broke one of them," he said.

We talked for a brief time and as he looked into my eyes, it became clear to him that I was not the "devil" he assumed me to be.

I noticed his display of pictures, magazine photos, and the murals he had drawn on his cell wall. I told him I admired his cell arrangement and added, "I'm really sorry you hurt your hand. I'm sorry you're in jail."

The love of God that the prison guard and I demonstrated to him brought about a dramatic transformation to his countenance. He was now apologetic for the words he had shouted and took one of his prized magazine pictures off the wall and offered it to me as a gift.

Inmates are only allowed a Bible and one other book in our cells. Magazines and newspapers are not allowed. This man was giving me one of his most prized possessions, a magazine collage of trees, mountains, oceans, and birds.

When I entered the Three South Cluster to take a shower, the devil tried to unleash a tirade against me. Before I left, the Holy Spirit had worked a miracle in this man.

Returning to my cell, I spent time in prayer, asking the Holy Spirit to heal his emotional and physical injuries. Most of all, I thanked Him for enabling me to soothe the hurt and pain of this young man by walking in the love of God.

A gentle answer turns away wrath, but a harsh word stirs up anger.

PROVERBS 15:1

Robert Yates, Jr. is on death row at the state penitentiary in Walla Walla, Washington. Since his incarceration, he has accepted Jesus as his Lord and Savior. He is a murderer whose heart was transformed by the healing and renewing love of Jesus Christ. He ministers to his fellow inmates whenever a door opens.

41

THE BURNING BUSH

by Patrick Savage

$\mathcal{O}$n a beautiful autumn day in 2001, the chill of Old Man Winter filled the air. I decided to take a couple of days off from work to winterize our home and to complete a few other projects around the house. Although I usually head out the door at 4:45 A.M., my alarm went off at 6 A.M. on my day off. Normally this would be a treat. On this particular morning, however, I woke up exhausted.

It's rare for me to have trouble sleeping. My work in the maintenance department of an elementary school is physically demanding. When I climb into bed at night, I'm usually asleep as soon as my head hits the pillow.

I told my wife, Mary, that I had a restless night's sleep. We visited a short while before she left for work. As she was heading out the door, we made arrangements to meet for lunch. We rarely have the opportunity to do this. I work across town and only have a half-hour for lunch. We decided to take advantage of the day and arranged to meet at noon. Before I met Mary, I had to stop by the school and pick up my keys from the substitute they brought in to cover my duties.

A couple of hours later as I was preparing to leave to pick up the keys, I heard a distinct voice in my spirit say, "Don't go!" This seemed rather unusual to me. I wasn't quite sure what to make of it, so I shrugged if off and continued to get ready to leave. Once again I heard a voice say, "Don't go!" Since I didn't need my keys until the weekend, I decided not to leave.

After finishing up some projects around the house, I walked down the hallway to the bathroom to wash my hands. The bathroom lights began to flicker, and I heard a strange crackling noise.

Looking out the window, I saw one of our eight-foot shrubs next to the house engulfed in flames. I ran out of the house in my stocking feet and jumped off the deck near the shrub. In order to reach the water faucet, I had to crawl between the burning shrub and the shrub next to it. I knew there was no time to go back into the house to call 911. If I did, the house would surely catch on fire.

I grabbed the hose and started spraying the shrub. As the smoke billowed from the yard, I was certain that one of our neighbors would see the smoke and flames and call the fire department. I fought the blaze until the fire was extinguished.

I examined the side of the house, the gutters, and the shingles on the roof to find out the extent of the damage. There wasn't any, not even a single smudge of smoke!

Confident the fire had been contained, I called Mary and said, "I'm going to be late. Our house almost burnt down, and I just put out the fire."

After telling her the story, she asked me if I knew how the shrub caught on fire. I didn't know. After hanging up the phone with Mary, I called the utility company to request an inspection of our power lines. When the utility company representative arrived, he examined the power lines and soon discovered the cause of the fire.

One of the oak trees in our back yard had grown into the wires of the main power line to our house. As the wind blew, the tree rubbed against the power line, eventually wearing off the protective coating. After the line was bare and as the tree continued to rub against it, sparks began to fly and drop into the shrub.

The utility man looked me in the eye and said, "Do you realize how lucky you were to be home when this happened? If you had not been here, your house would have caught fire. You could have lost everything.

Hearing his words, I remembered the voice I heard that morning. The hair on the back of my neck stood up as I realized what could have happened and shuddered at the thought of losing everything.

I believe the reason I was so restless the night before the fire was because my spirit knew what was about to happen. Realizing how God protected us, I began to praise and thank Him for protecting our home.

I am thankful that I obeyed God's voice. This near tragedy made me realize that our prayers of protection over our home and family were answered that day.

I was late for my lunch date with Mary. I was quite hungry when I finally arrived and don't think I've ever enjoyed such a delicious Reuben sandwich. Mary even picked up the tab!

The prudent see danger and take refuge, but the simple keep going and suffer for it.

PROVERBS 27:12

Patrick Savage is a maintenance worker in the Mead School District in Spokane, Washington. He coaches basketball and is an avid hockey fan. His wife, Mary, and their daughter enjoy camping and any other activity where they can share time together.

42

OVERRULED BY GOD'S REPORT
by Tim Diaz

In 1997 my wife and I were in a church service when our pastor gave us a word that changed our lives. He first gave us encouraging words about our ministry and then prophesied that my wife would become pregnant. Although we had three children from our previous marriages, we had none together. Because we had tried for some time to have children, we welcomed the news of a future child. However, we did not fully understand one portion of the prophecy. After assuring us that we would have a child, he added, "Don't listen to what the doctors say."

My wife soon became pregnant but suffered a miscarriage in her third month. In a second pregnancy, she began to hemorrhage in her fourth month. She bled so profusely that I feared she would die. Although doctors stopped the bleeding, they were unable to find the baby's heartbeat. We lost our second child.

Three months later, doctors discovered a tumor in my testicle. Recommending surgical removal of the tumor and possible chemotherapy, they explained that the treatment would leave me sterile.

Facing cancer, my faith wavered. I had to seek the Lord for answers. Although I knew of God's ability to heal, I had seen Christians die from cancer.

"How can I know if I will survive this cancer?" I asked Him.

God spoke to my spirit. "Tim, do you beat your wife?"

What does that have to do with cancer? I thought to myself.

He asked again, "Do you beat your wife?"

"No, Lord, I love my wife and wouldn't do anything to hurt her."

"I don't beat My wife either," God assured me. "You and My church are My bride. I didn't do this to you. Satan is a wife beater, not Me."

I became fully persuaded that Satan authored this disease and wanted to take my life. God wanted me to enjoy an abundant, healthy life. With the revelation that Jesus was my Healer, I was prepared to fight spiritually.

On the day of my surgery, the nurse in pre-op asked if I wanted medication to calm me. Because I had already found peace through prayer, I declined. She asked if she could pray for me before surgery, telling me that she and two other doctors involved in the procedure were believers. "Of course you can pray!" I told her.

While I was in surgery, my wife and a close friend also prayed for my healing.

God answered all of their prayers. When I regained consciousness, my wife was waiting to exclaim, "Jesus healed you!"

"What do you mean?" I asked.

She exuberantly explained, "The doctor is dumbfounded. He couldn't find the tumor even though it was present in pre-op. When they made the incision to remove the tumor, it was gone!"

We knew why the cancer could not be found—Jesus healed me!

Tissue samples from the location of the tumor were sent to three different universities for evaluation. All tests showed that the samples were benign.

We also have another miracle, a beautiful baby girl. By choosing to place our faith in the unchanging truth of God's Word instead of a doctor's report, we found victory over disease.

The thief comes only to steal and kill and destroy; I have come that they may have life, and have it to the full.

JOHN 10:10

Tim Diaz was born in Farmington, New Mexico. A Christian for 30 years, he is blessed with a beautiful wife and four children.

43

"IF YOU DID IT FOR THEM,
YOU CAN DO IT FOR ME"
by Mary Hill

In 1979 my two children and I moved to an apartment shortly after I filed for divorce. I worked part-time while trying to clean up the mess my life had become.

One weekend all three of us were suffering from a stomach flu. I felt physically drained and weakened after vomiting throughout the day. During the birth of my first child, I developed an illness known as Sheehan's Syndrome, which requires that I receive daily hydrocortisone shots and Synthroid® to assist with glandular insufficiency.

I didn't know it at the time, but if I am sick, I need a shot of cortisone to supply my body with the necessary amount of adrenaline that my glands do not produce. Without the shot I run the risk of going into a low blood sugar coma.

That evening I put the children to bed and fell asleep. I awoke confused and disoriented. Although lightheaded, I managed to find my way to the phone and call my mother. I hung up the phone, passed out, fell, and hit my head. My mother arrived with the police. They found me semiconscious on the floor by my bed.

The next day my doctor diagnosed me with a concussion and ordered a battery of tests. A neurosurgeon later met with me to discuss the results. He said I fractured my skull when I fell and x-rays showed that I had a brain hemorrhage. They also discovered a foreign mass and suspected that it was a tumor that must be surgically removed. He also felt it would be necessary to drill a hole in my skull to drain the blood from the hemorrhage.

I was hospitalized immediately and scheduled for surgery the following day. The doctor ordered a few more tests as a formality prior to surgery but was focused on removing the mass from my brain.

Grabbing my Bible in the hospital, I started reading about the miracle healings that Jesus performed throughout His ministry. I prayed, "Lord, You healed all of these people in the Bible. If You did it for them, You can do it for me."

That night my mom, a priest, my brothers, and a friend of the family laid hands on me and asked God to heal me.

The following morning I was taken downstairs for more tests in nuclear medicine. Afterward I met with a puzzled surgeon. "The mass has disappeared," he said. His inability to understand the disappearance of the mass in my brain made him angry.

"My family and friends laid hands on me last night and asked God to heal me. That's why the mass disappeared," I explained.

Looking at me in bewilderment, he said, "I don't know."

The surgery was cancelled, and I was released from the hospital in good health.

Although my life was a broken mess at the time, my simple prayer of faith healed me.

Is any one of you sick? He should call the elders of the church to pray over him and anoint him with oil in the name of the Lord.

> *And the prayer offered in faith will make the sick person well; the Lord will raise him up. If he has sinned, he will be forgiven.*
>
> JAMES 5:14,15

Mary Hill has lived in Eastern Washington her entire life. She graduated from Gonzaga University in the seventies and works in social services. Mary has three children and was recently married to her new husband, Tim.

44

REQUIEM FOR A HEAVYWEIGHT
by Bob Boardman

*P*inned down on Peleliu's "Orange Beach Three," the marines were trapped in a terrifying, living hell with no apparent way out. The great majority of them were teenagers. It was September 15, 1944, the first hour after landing on this six-by-three mile coral outcropping in the Palau Islands, part of the Caroline Islands in the Pacific.

The Japanese defenders had the beach zeroed in with devastatingly accurate mortar fire. Machine-gun, anti-boat, and anti-tank fire from concealed pillboxes, coconut log, and concrete bunkers also swept over the embattled marines like rain from an angry and ceaseless typhoon.

On top of this came artillery fire from many of the 500 camouflaged caves and fortifications inside the ominous and dominant ridge on the island called Umurbrogal, renamed Bloody Nose Ridge by the marines. These hidden guns rained down shellfire to join the awesome crescendo pulverizing the young Leathernecks on the beach.

Torn bodies and body parts were strewn among the living. It would be only a matter of time before the remainder of A Company, 1st Battalion, Seventh Marine Regiment of the First Marine Division joined their dead and dying comrades.

Charles "Chick" Owen, a sixteen-year-old private, couldn't believe that he would wind up on this beachhead. This was not the romantic, exciting picture he had imagined when he lied about his age and joined the marines two years earlier when he was fourteen. He was positive that he and others, petrified with fear, would never survive.

Peleliu was one of the bloodiest of the Marine Corps fifteen major amphibious landings in the Pacific during World War II. The Japanese had 10,000 to 13,000 fanatical defenders; no one knows the exact number. They exacted from the First Marine Division 1,121 killed, 5,142 wounded, and 73 missing in action—a total of 6,336 casualties. In addition, the U.S. Army's 81st Wildcat Division sustained 542 killed and 2,028 wounded on Peleliu and Angaur. Most of Colonel Nakagawa's defending contingent was killed in the approximate one-month battle.

Nakagawa's commanding officer, Lieutenant General Sadae Inoue, commanded all 40,000 defending Imperial Japanese Army and Navy troops in Palau Island. He followed Japan's ancient code of Bushido, the way of the Warrior, by attempting to instill this philosophy into every man before the marines landed. He issued an edict called "Training for Victory." Spiritual discipline is placed first on the list of requirements to inflict defeat on the enemy in the upcoming battle. "We must first resolutely penetrate the enemy, and then we shall display our short swords and slash his bones to the very marrow," declared Inoue.

This was the fanatical enemy that opposed the marine beachhead on Peleliu. Private Owen describes the landing: "I was in one of the first waves. When we hit the beach, I went over the side of the amphib tractor. It was a long jump and felt like falling into hell."

I asked Owen if he prayed as he was pinned down in the sand in that indescribable scene. He replied. "I can safely say everyone on that beach prayed, either desperately to themselves or out loud."

Onto this scene of sand and coral carnage and out of the smoke and haze of this confusion, death, and destruction strode another marine. Could this Leatherneck officer, armed with a tommy-gun and with a Japanese shovel slung over his shoulder, be an answer to these desperate men's prayers?

This outwardly fearless, mysterious figure wore his major's insignia in plain sight rather than hidden on the underside of his collar to not attract enemy snipers. His amphibious tank had been hit on the way in and had caught fire. It had to be abandoned by the major and his crew. One man was killed.

As the major strode up the beach, he saw Owen and the congregated group of frozen Marines, unable to move from fear. All combat marines had been trained to not remain on a beach because of the extreme danger. To Owen, the only alternative was to rush into the face of enemy fire and that did not look so inviting. To stand up in the midst of that maelstrom seemed like certain death. Yet here was the unknown major doing just that.

Chick Owen described what happened. "The noise of the incoming fire was so loud that voice contact was almost impossible. The artillery, anti-tank, mortar, machine gun, and other small arms fire was dealing out wholesale death upon the assaulting marines, particularly to those who chose to remain on the beach. I heard a very loud, booming voice, one that could be heard above the noises of battle, one I will never forget. It still rings in my ears today. 'Get off this beach or I'll shoot your butt!'"

Most men on a fire-swept beach would crouch over and attempt to scurry to their next position. Not the major. He stood upright.

His commanding presence and booming voice served to release those young lads. This was clearly double jeopardy—the wrath and threats of the unknown major or the Japanese mortars. The choice was easy. They jumped up and moved inland on the double!

Later, Owen learned that the next mortar barrage exploded precisely where they had been laying! "If that major hadn't been on that beach, I would have died right there, at age sixteen."

Charles Owen and his outfit moved inland taking bloody yard after hard won yard from the enemy who had pledged to fight to the death. That same night those persistent Japanese mortar shells, unable to find Owen on the beach, caught up with him. Wounded slightly in the neck, he was evacuated to a hospital ship for a short time but soon rejoined what remained of A-1-7 and finished out the battle of Peleliu.

Owen served the Marine Corps for well over 22 years, went through three wars, and retired as a master sergeant. During all of those years and long after his retirement, he often wondered who the mysterious major was that he encountered so briefly on the beach at Peleliu. Who was this mud-smeared, bloodied officer who had become an answer to the desperate prayers of so many of his fellow marines in the midst of death and dying?

Throughout all of Charles Owen's battles and experiences in the Corps, which include Okinawa, North China, Korea, and Vietnam, he testifies, "I have seen many deeds of heroism in combat but none even closely compare with the performance of that major on the beach at Peleliu."

Finally, through a set of what could only be described as God-given circumstances, all of the pieces to the puzzle finally fit together. The mysterious, unknown major was identified. W.H. "Brock" Brockinton, a marine rifle platoon and a company commander in the battle of Okinawa, read Charles Owen's account in Bill Ross's book *Peleliu: Tragic Triumph*. Brock immediately knew that the unknown major was his close friend from Charleston, South Carolina, Arthur M. Parker Jr., lieutenant colonel, USMCR, retired!

It took 48 years to identify Arthur "Ace" Parker as the hero on that beachhead! Here is his response: "I was trying to get things back together on the beach when I ran into the infantry. There was a whole conglomeration of troops in one place, which was an easy target for the Japanese artillery and mortars. These infantrymen had to be removed from that beach or they would all be killed. To think that I would be remembered after all these years because of this incident makes my whole life worthwhile."

The desperate, sincere prayers for deliverance offered by young Charles Owen and his mostly teenage buddies on Peleliu's fire-swept Orange Beach were unexpectedly answered by the appearance of Ace Parker, a God-fearing man. The beach-strolling major disregarded his own safety. He was willing to put himself in great jeopardy, even to sacrifice his own life, to help inexperienced young marines live to continue the fight.

Hear my prayer, O Lord; listen to my cry for mercy.

In the day of my trouble I will call to you, for you will answer me.

PSALM 86:6,7

Robert Boardman entered the Marine Corps when he was eighteen and served in three major battles in World War II. During the Battle of Okinawa, he was shot in the neck. Thirty-three years later, God took him back to Okinawa to minister to his former enemy. Bob is the author of A Higher Honor *and* Unforgettable Men in Unforgettable Times.

45

LOOK MOM, IT'S GONE!

by Cheryl Gade

In 1993 we had moved from Minnesota to Spokane, Washington, after my husband accepted a management position at a craft store. Our first summer was filled with getting our new house in order, finding a school for the boys, and locating a good church.

The bold messages taught by our new pastor caused us to act on our beliefs and be "doers" of the Word. (James 1:22.) Faith seemed new and fresh to us as we discovered a deeper walk with God.

Bedtime has always been precious to our family. One storybook often turned into two or three. After reading a Bible story, the boys cleverly offered their personal translation of the story by adding unique details. Sweet voices prayed for blessings, hugs and kisses were shared, little bodies were tucked in, and the lights were turned off.

One night while kissing my youngest cherub, Douglas, I noticed a bubble at the base of his teeth. With the growing experience of raising three rambunctious boys, I did not panic over the unexpected find but decided to keep an eye on the growth that made its home in my son's mouth.

I examined Douglas's mouth nightly. The bubble consistently grew until it caused his lip to protrude. We questioned him with growing concern. "Does it hurt? Can you move it with your tongue? Does it bother you?"

Douglas had developed into a "tough" little boy by having two older brothers. Though only three, he knew how to handle the rough stuff. Ear infections never bothered him and fever did not slow him down. This new challenge provoked no bother or worry to my young lad. I, on the other hand, was concerned enough to pursue a solution.

Being new to the city, we asked around to locate a trustworthy dentist. After a quick examination, we were ushered into the dentist's office. "I've never seen anything like this before," the doctor said with concern.

We were immediately referred to another dentist that could surgically remove the growth. They planned to anesthetize Douglas, then biopsy the bubble once it was removed.

My thoughts reeled. *He's only three, Lord. I don't want him to have surgery. We don't even have insurance yet.* Gathering up my innocent child who knew nothing of the fear that descended on his mother, we headed to see his father at work.

My detailed report to Scott was solemn. "Call and schedule the surgery," he offered as a logical conclusion. "We have to get this taken care of." I knew Scott well enough to know he was equally concerned about Douglas, yet he stood strong to carry me through my weak moment.

Hearing our dilemma, the assistant manager spoke up, "Well, we'll just believe that he'll be fine, in Jesus' name. God will take good care of him!"

We stared at her in wonderment. Faith! I was quickly reminded that faith was more powerful than any sickness or disease that would attempt to place itself on our child.

That night, bedtime was sweet as always. However, after the Bible story, Scott took control of our prayer time. "We're going to pray for Douglas's mouth," he said with authority.

We had learned from the Scripture that if someone is sick, we could lay hands on him and pray in faith for his healing. Douglas's two older brothers bound out of bed, jumped onto Douglas's bed, and laid their little hands on their brother. Scott placed his hand on his chin and prayed a simple prayer of faith while I stroked his hair. After hugs and kisses, the boys jumped into bed, and the lights went out.

The next day was bright and sunny. Waking the boys for the new day, I took a few minutes to rub backs and tousle hair. When Douglas welcomed me with a bear hug, I quickly asked him if I could look inside his mouth as I had done each morning for many days.

Douglas dutifully pulled down his lip on one side revealing a pink, healthy gum line. *Hmm,* I thought. *It must be the other side.* He pulled down the lip on the other side. I saw nothing.

"Douglas, open your mouth wide," I commanded. Inspecting his mouth as a buyer would inspect a horse, I found no abrasion, scar, or redness, only clear, pink gum tissue. The ugly looking bubble had completely disappeared.

Smothering my baby with hugs, he squirmed to get loose. While I celebrated our miracle, Douglas's attention was already focused on breakfast.

> *...take up the shield of faith, with which you can extin-guish all the flaming arrows of the evil one.*
>
> EPHESIANS 6:16

Cheryl Gade divides her time between three active young boys, her husband, work at a local church, and the Healing Room Ministries in Spokane, Washington. She is strengthened by a lifelong personal walk with Jesus Christ and loves to share the miraculous way God moves in her life with those around her.

46

GOOD GROUND

by Lloyd C. Phillips

For years I suffered from chronic, degenerating knees and was in constant discomfort and pain. My condition concerned me, not only because I teach and minister supernatural healing, but because I also enjoy hiking and hunting in the mountains.

In the fall of 1999, I was ministering in a church in Colorado, teaching about the gifts of the Holy Spirit, including the gifts of healing.

I explained to the congregation that the gifts of the Spirit are given to us by God to use for the benefit of others and not to keep for ourselves. I further explained that many healing evangelists have witnessed dramatic miracles of healing, yet struggled with health problems themselves or with their family members.

I believe that after a person receives a miracle, he or she should "give back" to someone else in need. I believe those who have received a healing should pray for the minister who laid hands on him or her so the minister can also receive any needed miracle.

I then demonstrated how to pray for the sick. As I was praying for people in the congregation, a woman came up to me and asked if I was experiencing any problems in my legs.

"Yes," I replied.

"I knew that God was telling me about your legs!" she exclaimed and then turned to walk away.

"Hey, wait a minute," I stopped her. "You've received a word of knowledge from God. You now have the responsibility to pray for me."

She asked her friend who had come to the service with her to pray with her. I sat down in a chair and asked the pastor to pray with them. I never told them that my knees were giving me problems. At one point, however, one of them began to pray specifically for the healing of my knees.

Immediately, both kneecaps became like liquid. They were soft and pliable. Everyone knows that kneecaps are stiff and firm, but mine became like a bowl of Jell-O.

I said to the pastor, "Look! I'm getting new kneecaps." They gasped as they realized that something supernatural was happening.

"Put your hand on my knee and feel this," I said.

When the miracle was completed, I jumped up and down, did some deep knee bends, and praised the Lord.

I took advantage of my healing the next day. I went for a long hike in the mountains. I can honestly say my "new knees" wore out my "old legs." I have never been in pain again, not from that day to this.

> And it shall come to pass in that day, that his burden shall be taken away from off thy shoulder, and his yoke from off thy neck, and the yoke shall be destroyed because of the anointing.
>
> ISAIAH 10:27 KJV

Lloyd Phillips is a full-time minister in Missoula, Montana. He is the director of FLInt Net, Fellow Laborer's International Network, an association of ministers and ministries joined together to fulfill the Great Commission.

47

IT'S TOO LOUD!

by Geri Copper

In January of 1995, our church invited Pastor Duane Swilley from Atlanta, Georgia, to share the Word of God with us. God used him mightily while he was there. The lives of many people in our congregation were changed, including my youngest son, Billy.

The change in Billy was phenomenal. I prayed that the rest of my household would take notice and return to the Lord. I especially prayed for my husband, Terry.

When I learned that Pastor Swilley was returning to our church, I wrote him a letter asking that he would pray that God would either heal my husband's ears or that God would provide the necessary finances to buy hearing aids before he arrived. "It won't do any good for Terry to come to the service if he can't hear what you're saying," I wrote.

When Pastor Swilley returned in May, we had not been able to purchase the hearing aids, and Terry's hearing had not improved. We strategically sat in the second row on the right-hand side of the church, which enabled Terry to sit at an angle and cup the back of his ear to hear what was being said.

When the service began, Pastor Swilley noticed what he was doing. He pointed to him and asked, "What do you want God to do for you?"

Terry leaned over to me and asked, "What did he say?"

I repeated what was said. Terry looked at Pastor Swilley and said, "I want to hear you!"

He then instructed Terry to come up to the front row and asked for our pastors to gather around him. Pastor Swilley put his hands over Terry's ears and carefully placed a finger in each ear. He prayed for the power of God to heal Terry. When Pastor Swilley gently pulled his fingers away, the look on Terry's face was indescribable. He grabbed his ears and began to cry.

"What's wrong?" Pastor Swilley asked.

Terry replied, "It's too loud!" The congregation roared with laughter and praise.

Not only were Terry's ears changed, but his heart was changed as well. Before his healing, he didn't want anything to do with people. He would just as soon bite a person's head off as to give him or her the time of day.

Terry often says, "You wouldn't have liked me before I was healed."

I believe that a lot of his anger resulted from his inability to hear. It always angered him when people talked to him from behind or with their backs turned away from him.

Terry's heart had also been captivated by worldly things, which kept him from loving others and worshiping the Lord. His heart now is aflame with love and filled with compassion for the Lord.

There some people brought to him a man who was deaf and could hardly talk, and they begged him to place his hand on the man

...Jesus put his fingers in the man's ears....

He looked up to heaven and with a deep sigh said to him, "Ephphatha!" (which means, "Be opened!").

At this, the man's ears were opened, his tongue was loosened and he began to speak plainly.

MARK 7:32-35

Geri and Terry Copper met while in their senior year of high school and were married one year and three days later in 1969. Terry is a deacon at Living Hope Church in Coeur d'Alene, Idaho. Terry blows the shofar (a ram's horn that is blown at Jewish celebrations) at their church services and wherever God leads him.

48

THE BIG FIRE
by Esther Estacion

*O*n Saturday, January 14, 2000, around four o'clock in the morning, my husband woke up needing a drink of water. As he walked down the hall, he heard a loud noise outside the house. He went to the window closest to where the sound was coming from and saw the building next door on fire.

The wooden building was an old, large, two-story structure. No one lived in it. The Catholic church owned it, and priests stored auto repair machines and school items that they no longer used in the building.

The fire raged through the building, quickly devouring everything in it. Cesar screamed for us to get up. We grabbed whatever we could gather and scrambled out of our house before it also burned down. The two dwellings were very close to each other, only seven meters separated the buildings.

My husband and I were so rattled that we couldn't think. I whispered a prayer to God, "Please help me know what to do." I spread a blanket over our clothes and ran outside to safety.

By the time we reached the street, many of the townspeople were out front watching the fire. "There's no hope for your house," they yelled to us. "Get away from it!"

I knew that God had given us this place and that He would protect us from trouble. In front of all the townspeople I shouted,

"God, show these people that You are able to deliver us from this fire. Perform a miracle and save us."

I watched as my family and students from the Bible school fought the fire with garden hoses, trying to keep it from spreading. Almost immediately, the building crashed to the ground, and the fire began to burn slower. It was as though an angel stood between our home and the fire. The hot flames never touched our home, nor did it burn or melt the plastic fence only a meter from the burning building.

Within a very short time, the fire was completely out. The fire department arrived too late to help, and we safely returned to our home.

The building next door turned into a heap of ashes. The neighbors and people who watched the fire could not believe that our home was spared.

They saw that God is able to protect those who call on Him. That morning news of the fire was broadcast over the radio. One caller asked, "What happened to the house next door? Did it burn down as well?"

"No, it wasn't touched," said the reporter. "It's still there."

We were very wet and dirty after the fire. Some of us washed and cleaned ourselves in basins upstairs, others downstairs. It was early morning, so instead of going back to bed, I cooked breakfast.

Since we were married, we had gotten in the habit of "eating" God's Word before we ate our breakfast. While my husband was reading the devotional to us, he burst into tears. Soon, everyone was shedding tears of thanksgiving. If it were not for God's protection, we would not be sitting at our table peacefully listening to His Holy Word that morning. What a great God we have!

The Lord is near to all who call on him, to all who call on him in truth.

He fulfills the desires of those who fear him; he hears their cry and saves them.

PSALM 145:18,19

Esther is co-pastor of the Tagbilaran Baptist Church on the Island of Bohol in the Philippines. She and her husband, Cesar, were educated at the Baptist Theological College in Cebre. Esther oversees church conferences, camps, weddings, and funerals, translates materials into their native language, and trains graduates from their Bible school.

49

TO DEATH AND BACK
by Paul Hughes

In September 1969 the infantry unit I served with received orders to return to Tam Ky, South Vietnam. Two months earlier the U.S. lost an entire platoon there in an early morning ambush. We were ordered to relieve the Echo Company because of the heavy losses they had taken as a result of land mines and booby traps.

My outfit, the Alpha Company, had been in the jungle for three weeks and was scheduled for a couple of days bunker duty at our firebase, LZ Baldy. To us, Baldy was a resort. At least we could take an occasional shower and eat a decent meal. Bunker duty was luxurious compared to the canopy jungle of the Central Highlands. However, Echo Company needed to be pulled out of the field, and it became our lot to relieve them.

Tam Ky was saturated with hidden explosives armed to detonate on contact. During my seven months in Vietnam, I witnessed a lot of death. Now we were about to walk straight into death's living room.

Our company was tired and frustrated. When we realized where we were going, we also became frightened. We put on our flak jackets, resupplied, and moved out to the chopper pad for the airlift to Tam Ky.

After touching down, we camped outside the city for the night. Along with the darkness came a monsoon rain. The water striking our canvas ponchos drowned out any attempt to communicate, and the moisture brought with it a cold, unearthly feeling. We spent the night soaking wet and waited for a morning that none of us looked forward to seeing. We knew that death was imminent but had no way of knowing for whom.

Early in the morning on September 9 we cautiously proceeded through the underbrush near a village on the edge of a rice field. I was in the second platoon and was probably the twentieth man in the column. The falling rain seemed endless as the dark, foreboding sky set the stage for death and disaster. A deafening explosion on the point echoed throughout the area and suddenly the quiet was eroded with the battlefield cry for help, "Medic, Medic!"

I rushed to the front of the column. Men half dead, limbs missing, cried out to God for help. We quickly set up an area for the medivac choppers. The nightmarish color of blood saturated the wounded soldiers' drab olive green army jungle fatigues. An African-American soldier with his stomach blown open called for his mother and died as we lay him down for evacuation.

We were able to airlift the last of the dead and wounded an hour before dark. We now had fifteen less men than at the beginning of the day. The remaining men started to dig foxholes around the edge of our perimeter. My assignment as a grenadier was to stay in the center of the perimeter with the commanding officer and his radiotelephone operator. I removed the heavy flak jacket and my helmet and heated some water for coffee. It had been a very tense day.

For the third time I reread a letter from home, probably for sanity's sake. One of my friends was digging his foxhole at the edge of our defense perimeter, and I thought we might chat for a moment.

"Hey Dave," I called out as I sat near a bomb crater heating water. "Come here for a minute!" Dave stopped digging and headed my way as I continued to read the letter from my mother. He was a few yards to my right when he started to head toward me. When I glanced up, he was standing beside me.

I lowered my head to fold up the letter. Instantly, everything turned bright red. Even though I felt no pain, I somehow realized that I had left this world and had entered another realm. I didn't know at that point what happened, but I knew I had died and had entered the spirit realm. There's an old slogan among soldiers that says, *You'll never hear the one that gets you.* It had proven itself true in my life.

Realizing I had died, I wondered where I was headed next, to heaven or hell? For a quaint moment, I found myself assessing my life as if evaluating my qualifications for eternity.

Aware that I had no control over the situation I found myself at the entrance of a vast black tunnel that appeared endless. At the far distant end of the cylinder, I could see a brilliant, white light. I knew that my entrance into the light would finalize my eternal destination, although at this point I didn't know the final outcome.

I began to travel down the center of the tunnel at supersonic speed. Suddenly, I was at the far end of the tunnel about to enter into the brilliant, white light that only seconds ago seemed miles away. The realization that I was about to discover my eternal destination was overwhelming.

From my peripheral vision, I saw my entire life on the wall of the tunnel. Everything I had ever done covered the mysterious sides of the black cylinder that looked like a projection screen. I surveyed my life from all angles. I saw myself riding a tricycle as a small child right on up to the time that I was drafted only a few months earlier.

As I refocused on the brilliant light, I heard a clear, firm voice say, "Ask God to let you live." The voice expected an immediate answer.

Having been raised in a Southern Baptist family, I attended church as a youngster and certainly knew about God and Jesus Christ. I even had a vision of Jesus two months earlier during a night ambush. I believed in God and the afterlife but never thought that He would care enough to pay attention to a rascal like me. One thing I did know; I was sure that God could restore my life. Of that I had no doubt.

Realizing that I was running out of time and was about to exit the tunnel, I cried out, "God, please let me live; I don't want to die!" Three times I made my heartfelt cry. Suddenly, the scene changed.

Everything turned black. I (my spirit) was in complete darkness. My spirit was slowly floating farther and farther away, and it was becoming more difficult to see with each passing moment. When I could barely see my spirit anymore, a huge hand appeared in front of me. Even though I could see through the hand, it looked like a white glove. The hand clasped onto my spirit, brought it back to my body, and placed my spirit inside of my body.

I lifted my head, knowing that I had been badly wounded. The medics had left me for dead. My right eye was badly injured. As I turned to see what else might be wrong with me, I noticed my left combat boot was underneath my buttocks. My left leg had been blown apart just below the knee. I was saturated with my blood and the blood of my good friend.

"Medic!" I yelled. My hearing was gone, one eye blinded, and I had only one good leg. I needed immediate first aid and again called for a medic with all the strength I could muster.

Even though enemy assault was blasting on our position, the medic stayed by my side and injected me with morphine. He wrapped both of my eyes and dressed my other wounds as best he could. The medivac choppers were immediately dispatched but couldn't land because of the hostile fire. A gunship finally arrived laying down cover fire for our pick up.

As I was hoisted up into the chopper I cried out, "Did you get Dave?" As the chopper lifted, a strange voice replied to my nagging inquiry, "We got what we could find." I knew he must be dead and later found out that an incoming rocket hit him in the chest, killing him instantly.

Those were the last words I heard as I left the battlefield, lame, blind, and in shock from loss of blood. For some reason, beyond human logic, almighty God allowed me to live. And for that kindness, I will always serve Him.

You are my hiding place; you will protect me from trouble and surround me with songs of deliverance.

PSALM 32:7

Paul Hughes, author of The Light Within, *is a decorated Vietnam veteran. He is an ordained minister and lectures at colleges, churches, and schools. Paul has been a guest on numerous television programs and has been interviewed throughout the United States by both the Christian and secular media. He and his wife, Eva Louise, have one daughter.*

50

ANYBODY GOT A U-JOINT?
by Becky Weber

Several years ago my husband and I headed to Canada for a summer camping trip. Our getaway was a refreshing time for both of us. We enjoyed slow morning starts and leisurely walks through the woods. Watching the wildlife, seeing baby moose with their mother, and taking scenic trips through some of God's most beautiful country left us feeling revived and ready to return to the fast-paced lifestyle we had left. To complete our vacation, we planned to stop in Sandpoint, Idaho, to enjoy a nice dinner.

An hour from the Canadian border our truck started to make a terrible noise. Scott expressed concern that it sounded like the u-joint was about to go. "It'll cost over a thousand dollars for a new u-joint assembly to replace the old one," he said. We were in the middle of nowhere and didn't know how much farther we could travel in the failing condition of our truck.

I thought, *This is a guy thing. It's Scott's truck and is a problem I don't understand at all!* However, anticipation stirred in my heart. The Lord was up to something, and I needed to step back and watch.

I believed this was a miracle in the making for my husband and suspected that it was intended to bring a message of provision to him from God. I silently prayed as I waited to see what would happen next.

As we turned a corner, we approached a gas station, restaurant, and towing service. This oasis seemed to be part of a family business. The moment we turned the corner our truck died, and we coasted into this isolated haven of provision.

Although relieved to find help, I was disappointed that our trip was ending with such an expensive expenditure. If the u-joint was the cause of our problems, we knew it could take days to get it fixed. Perhaps we would have to leave our camper in Canada and find a ride home.

Our only option was to be towed to a body shop called Horrible Hank's in a nearby town. We spent the last night in the parking lot of Horrible Hank's and waited for Hank to open in the morning.

"Lord, I know You have a sense of humor, but Horrible Hank's? What in the world is going on?" I pleaded. "I thought Scott and I were going out to a nice dinner in Sandpoint to end our vacation. Now we've ended up in a body shop parking lot. What kind of place is this? Will it be safe? Why is it called Horrible Hank's? I know You're up to something, Father."

The next morning we were Horrible Hank's first customers. To our dismay the u-joint was irreparably damaged. Just as Scott suspected, it would be very costly to fix.

The customer service attendant looked through his parts catalogue looking for a used, less expensive u-joint assembly. There was none available. Our only option was to order a new u-joint with a thousand dollar plus price tag attached to it.

I didn't believe it was God's will for us to leave our truck in Canada and spend that kind of money on a part. I told Scott I was going back to the camper to wait. I got inside and prayed, "Father, please provide for our need as You've promised in Your Word."

When the camper door suddenly flung open, Scott stood there with a grin on his face. "You've been praying, haven't you?"

I smiled, waiting to hear about the miracle the Lord had done for us.

Behind the body shop was a small junkyard. In the middle of this wrecking heap was a u-joint assembly that was an exact match to the one we needed for our truck. The u-joint from the junkyard was cheap compared to ordering a new part. Within a half-hour, our truck was repaired, and we were on the road again.

Horrible Hank's turned out to be not so horrible after all. God knows exactly what kind of miracle we need to make our journey with Him exciting.

And my God will meet all your needs according to his glorious riches in Christ Jesus.

PHILIPPIANS 4:19

Becky Weber is the founder of Fragrance Ministries and has ministered for over 24 years in churches, women's groups, and retreats. She and her husband, Scott, have been married for 32 years. They have three children and seven grandchildren.

51

THE POWER OF PRAYER
by Rosalie Willis

*M*ary Fox Murphy, President, Christian Women's Outreach and International Prayer Network, and my friend writes, "Prayer changes things! Every praying Christian knows this is an absolute fact. However, with the help of technology, prayer itself is changing. With the advent of rapid communication delivery systems, prayer has entered a unified, worldwide dimension. E-mail and fax capabilities make it possible to send prayer requests around the world instantly. Thousand of intercessors can be praying for a critical situation within thirty minutes. When thousands or perhaps millions, networked in worldwide prayer, begin to beseech God for a critical, personal difficulty, a no-hope condition, or an international crisis, miracles begin to happen. Such was the case for Rosalie Willis from Post Falls, Idaho."*

I'm alive today because of global prayer. Treasured friends and strangers around the world took time out of their busy schedules to fervently pray for me as the Lord healed me of multiple strokes, three code blues, multiple seizures, paralysis, blindness, deafness, 10 hours of surgery, a month in the hospital, and as I learned to breathe, talk, and walk again.

A year and a half after my brush with death, I visited Israel for the Feast of Tabernacles. I met many from different parts of the world who, when they heard that I was Rosalie Willis, exclaimed, I was praying for you last year!" Then we'd hug, laugh, and praise God that we got to meet, that He answered their prayers, and that He's totally healed me!

On January 15, 1998, while packing for a conference in Yakima, Washington, a paisley pattern blocked the vision in my left eye as I was overcome by a sickening feeling of weakness. After resting for an hour, I seemed to be fine. Five days later, however, I returned from Yakima feeling extremely weak.

A speaking invitation on my answering machine requested that I come to Cove, Oregon. Because this trip was important to me, I made the five-hour trip alone by car.

Disturbing symptoms continued to plague me. As I lay in bed at night, I heard a gurgling sound in my neck. The weakness in my body increased, so I drove home a day early. Once home, weakness again consumed me. This time I had to grab hold of a chair to keep from falling. I promised myself I would see my doctor the next day.

The doctor wasn't available so a nurse practitioner examined me. She cleaned out my ears and told me that I had water on my eardrums. An antibiotic and antihistamine was prescribed, and I left. Later that day I saw more jagged, brilliantly colored lights even when my eyes were closed. But by the time I got home that day, the lights disappeared and I seemed normal.

That night two seizures flailed me about like a rag doll, flinging me to the floor. When I called the hospital, the doctor said, "Come in immediately." It was in the middle of the night and I was home alone. I knew it wasn't safe to drive myself to the hospital, so I agreed to call my doctor first thing in the morning. I also called friends from A Company of Women to pray.

On Wednesday, January 28, I went to the emergency room of the local hospital, knowing that something was drastically wrong with me. After describing my symptoms to the ER doctor, an MRI and a barrage of other tests were ordered.

The next day my daughter, Shanette, flew in from Seattle to stay with me in the hospital. Tests indicated a problem in my carotid artery. Assuming that the artery was clogged, the doctor scheduled me for surgery the following day.

I suffered a stroke at 5:00 in the morning. The hospital staff called a code blue. At the same time, the Lord woke women from A Company of Women and instructed them to pray for me. Three hours later I regained consciousness but was paralyzed, blind, deaf, and unable to speak or breathe on my own. Most of the alarming symptoms disappeared within hours. When the surgeon began to operate later that morning, he discovered that the artery wasn't clogged but was torn. I was bleeding internally.

While on the operating table, my heart stopped and code blue was called. They again brought me back. After five hours of reconstructive surgery, the surgeon broke the news to my family. "I've done all I can," he said. "There's not much hope."

Two hours later, I awoke in the ICU Recovery Unit only to hear my surgeon say, "We're taking her back in."

The monitors indicated that I wasn't responding properly. Another arduous five-hour surgery transpired. The surgeon approached my family a second time, giving some hope if only I could survive the night.

I woke up at 11 P.M. in ICU. I was on oxygen and had tubes extending from me in all directions. My face was so swollen that I was unrecognizable. The pain was unbearable.

Trying to bring the swelling down, they put a block of ice wrapped in a towel on my neck but the weight of the ice increased the pain. My dear Shanette brought packages of frozen peas in small plastic bags and rotated them throughout the night. It worked.

The Lord had also alerted precious intercessors around the world to pray for me.

After the initial crisis, my daughter, family, and friends had contacted intercessors across the U.S. and in international prayer networks around the world to pray. They were told that the next few days were critical to my survival. Shanette's loving 24-hour presence in my hospital room during my hospital stay was also critical to my survival. God gave her the wisdom to know what to do at the right time. I was stabilizing although I was still in critical condition.

Four days later I suffered a third stroke and a third code blue. Once again, they brought me back. God's people were praying, and His intercessors continued to carry me.

For almost a month, I wasn't allowed to sit up, get out of bed, shower, or wash my hair. Everything had to be done for me. I had to learn to breathe, talk, and walk again. The muscles and nerves in my left arm shut down for three months because of the swelling in my neck. The Lord miraculously brought complete restoration and use to that arm. When I was released a month later, my recovery amazed doctors.

During the second month of my recovery, Shanette commuted back and forth from Seattle. She worked three days a week and then spent the next four days caring for me. She scheduled around-the-clock care for me. Friends from A Company of Women came to my home for their appointed time of care but often stayed over to enjoy the love and fellowship of other dear friends. The house was always filled with loving, laughing, worshiping, and praying women. What a wonderful way to heal!

On Easter Sunday, April 12, 1998, the celebration of Jesus' resurrection became my day of resurrection as well. I attended church and rejoiced over my miraculous healing and restoration. The nurse who had cared for me in the hospital was also in the service that morning. At first she didn't recognize me because she had only seen me at death's door. When she realized who I was, her obvious shock of seeing my full recovery spread across her face. Others were stunned when they heard of my brushes with death, and their faith was strengthened as they witnessed my recovery.

A year and a half later I visited Israel for the Feast of Tabernacles. I met many people who, when they heard that I was Rosalie Willis, exclaimed, "I was praying for you last year!" We hugged, laughed, and praised God that we got to meet and that He answered their prayers!

God is still in the miracle-working business as we pray in one accord! Although I don't know how many people prayed, I'm fully persuaded that because of their faithfulness to intercede, I'm alive, restored, and able to continue this wonderful adventure of loving God and loving His people.

> *Surely he took up our infirmities and carried our sorrows, yet we considered him stricken by God, smitten by him, and afflicted.*

> *But he was pierced for our transgressions, he was crushed for our iniquities; the punishment that brought us peace was upon him, and by his wounds we are healed.*

> ISAIAH 53:4,5

Rosalie Willis is the founder and co-director of A Company of Women, a family of women's ministries coming together in the unity of God's love. She wrote and recorded music for all 150 psalms and authored three books, A Walk With Jesus, Walking on With Jesus, *and* The Singing Bride. *Rosalie lives in Post Falls, Idaho.*

52

AN AUDIBLE VOICE

by Linda Butler

When my son, Shane, was an infant, we were returning home from my first church meeting as a new Christian. Hundreds of people at the service were on fire and excited about the Lord. There was something in the air. I couldn't recognize it, but it felt good.

That night a Catholic nun prayed with me to speak in tongues, and I was thrilled to be able to speak in a new heavenly language. Because I knew so little about speaking in tongues, I thought I would lose it if I stopped praying. I, therefore, prayed in tongues all the way home.

I had never heard the audible voice of God before, but as I approached an intersection, I heard these words, "A fast approaching vehicle is coming up on your right." I did not have to stop on the street in which I was driving; however, the crossing traffic did.

I didn't take time to discern from where this message was coming, but I did know that it wasn't the way I spoke. I slammed on my brakes just in time to see a car cross in front of me driving at nearly 50 miles per hour! Had I not reacted when I did, the young driver would have crashed into my son.

Needless to say, I continued to speak in tongues all the way home. My mother did not know what to think because I only spoke in tongues the rest of the night up until I fell asleep.

All of them were filled with the Holy Spirit and began to speak in other tongues as the Spirit enabled them.

ACTS 2:4

Linda Butler was a U.S. champion gymnast in 1968. She taught more than 900 gymnast students in her studio on the East Coast before returning to her hometown of Spokane, Washington. She and her husband have often shared their skills in an exuberant husband and wife Messianic dance team.

53

STITCHES IN THE FINAL SEAM
by Laurie Klein

Thailand, 1996. A stranger on a rusted motorcycle roared into a cluster of cement houses. Stopping only long enough to drop off a pile of leaflets, he zoomed into the jungle and was never seen again.

Would I have behaved better if I had known this sooner?

Thailand, December 23, 2000. Although I'm in charge of tomorrow's Christmas celebration, I don't know when it starts. Nor do I know the order of events, whether we have enough food, or why several hundred Buddhists would bother to attend. Boredom? American cookies, perhaps?

Although alcohol usually keeps things lively in this jungle village, our mission team's western ways tickle all of the local funny bones. They call us farangs and often cackle in embarrassment over our efforts to fit in. We're here to assist a long-term missionary. My assignment? To supervise the Christmas pageant with next to nothing, in the middle of nowhere. I have three weeks to get it all done.

A rooster chorus announces each sultry 100-degree day. My morning alarm launches me into an icy shower. Tepid rice and bottled water follow. We worship amid chickens, curious children, and wrangling dogs. Despite hectic communal living, God speaks to me through tiny prayer windows, much like thread going through a needle's eye. I go through to get through.

Mostly, it's knots. I hit many snags and my patience often frays. While the missionary scours Bangkok shops for candy canes, our primitive septic system overflows. I enact elaborate pantomimes so our cook will hold dinner. Others locate the landlord and tell him what happened to the toilets. Although they both speak a little English, we suspect they're feigning ignorance. Given our performance, who wouldn't?

My previous experience as a director/producer means nothing here. My lists and schedules mystify the village people. I'm overseeing a talented young Thai with great program ideas, but teamwork looks as foreign to him as I do.

Unbelief dogs me. How can I help these people when I can't communicate, find an interpreter, or even fathom the local customs?

One task, however, delights me. My new friends help me create a life-size manger scene from cast-off pieces of lumber, rags, straw, old coconuts, and other oddities. In addition to the holy family, I've stitched and glued birds and geckos from orphaned socks and buttons. An old pillowcase stuffed with straw makes a jolly pig. The village urchins finger everything I've created. *I'm glad the creche intrigues them. Really.* If I could be honest with you, on the days that I must reassemble everything all over again, Rhett Butler's words echo inside of me, "Frankly, my dear...."[1]

Crises pop up like toadstools after rain. The motorcycle's gone when we need it. The electrician doesn't show up.

I used to be so good at this! Still, I know that God has sent me here, and His grace threads through every glitch. He must be making a crazy quilt.

"You can only do what He asks," I tell myself. "Love the ones you're with and try to live in the moment that He's offering." What other choice do I have? They won't give me back my ticket; I already asked.

Because our costumer bailed out, I guard a borrowed stash of cloth, thirty precious safety pins, and two staplers. Tonight we'll costume the children backstage, although I still don't know who's playing what role. Surely the missionary will.

The actual event runs twelve hours. Quite chaotic, but the villagers love it. Our American games fascinate everyone. Between acts, tipsy students vie for the stage. A local singer makes amazing sounds. *I wonder if you need a license to sing like that.* She sings a long time. The mayor joins in. We clap and clap.

When the temperature drops, restless kids torch the field during the Christmas story. While I'm frantically stapling children into costumes, several appear with familiar cloth. They've ransacked my manger scene! They want to wear those costumes for the birth of Jesus, which I guess is okay, but torn between tears and wanting to hurt someone, I go into hiding as soon as I decently can and then creep home to bed.

Christmas day dawns anyway. I know I don't deserve it. When an eccentric village woman, who has regularly teased us by holding her knife to our throats, gives her life to Christ, guilty tears ambush me. She says that we love her more than her eight children, so Jesus must be worth knowing. Amazing.

Christmas night the local singer returns and baffles us all as she, too, prays with the missionary to become a Christian. When a few team members and a translator drive her back to her village to explain her conversion to her husband, I'm almost too tired to care. I just want to go home, but they have the only car.

Two hours later they jubilantly return. Since so little happens here, half of the village followed the missionary's car on foot, jammed into the singer's house to hear the good news, and prayed to be saved!

Miraculous? Yes, but remember that mysterious man on the motorcycle? It was the singer's tiny village he zoomed into, leaving dozens of tracts, then disappeared without explanation. They had never heard about Jesus. Wonderfully patient, the people saved those precious little booklets and waited for someone to show them how to walk in faith.

That's where we came in. Four years later, God sent a talented team halfway around the world to show us His garment of salvation already in the making. He allowed us to add a few small stitches in the final seam—even cranky, artistically-frustrated me.

Since returning to the States, several more villagers have converted, including our cook and the delightful singing mayor. My ideas of evangelism are forever altered. It has so little to do with my gifts or experience and everything to do with His love.

> ..."All authority in heaven and on earth has been given to me.
>
> Therefore go and make disciples of all nations, baptizing them in the name of the Father and of the Son and of the Holy Spirit, and teaching them to obey everything I have commanded you."
>
> MATTHEW 28:18-20

Laurie Klein adores her family and her ongoing studies in art, writing, theatre, music, and movement. She has authored the praise chorus "I Love You, Lord." If granted three wishes today, she would choose to love well, live in the moment, and the third...sorry, it's a secret!

54

"240" GORDY

by Chuck Dean

I'll never forget the time when "240" Gordy got saved. He was the type of guy who was always mad as a hornet. He showed up one year at a Vietnam veterans' family campout with his girlfriend and infant son looking for "something."

Some say he got the name "240" because he rode his Harley on a tavern bar in the Pacific Northwest. Supposedly the tavern's name was the "240-Mile Tavern." Others claim that he was called that because he weighed 240 pounds...none of which was fat.

He was a redheaded giant, a cross between a biker, a logger, and a marauding Viking from Norseland. The red hair and beard flowed over his chest and shoulders, and his steel blue eyes held a hurt that only another Vietnam vet could understand.

He didn't know what to make of the Christians singing around the campfire the first night of the campout. He stood back in the trees when the large circle of veterans began to pray. I wondered what he was doing here; but like many 'Nam vets, I thought he probably just wanted to hang out with the "brothers."

About midnight on the second night, Gordy was headed toward the latrine and came across a 'Nam vet who had surrendered his life to Christ. They struck up a conversation about Vietnam and really hit it off. About an hour later he prayed to give his heart to Jesus.

Everyone has a different experience when they become born again. For Gordy, from the moment he turned his life over to Christ, his life went into fast-forward. For the rest of the weekend, he had a glow about him that blessed our hearts. He even got water baptized in the ice-cold lake before he went home.

Gordy was born again on the 4th of July, Independence Day. This hardcore, 'Nam vet marine biker, celebrated a new kind of independence that weekend. For the first time since the war, he was free from the evil shadow of death that followed him wherever he went. He was now alive with Christ residing eternally in his heart. We were sure that we could hear a platoon of angels singing praise songs as they celebrated along with us.

The first thing Gordy did after becoming born again was to make Lauri an honest woman and give his son a proper name. He set the wedding date and recruited "Preacher Mike" to conduct the service. It was an awesome wedding and the first time I had ever been to a tent wedding with a biker preacher officiating. The whole place was surrounded by Harleys.

A few days after the wedding I was speaking at a church service attended mostly by Vietnam vets. Gordy was there. I spoke about the power that Satan holds over people through curses, charms, and witchcraft. As soon as I shed light on the "enemy," Gordy jumped up, ran to the altar, and wept uncontrollably.

I grabbed Gordy in a "brother's" hug. He told me how he had been set free again when I spoke those words and handed me what was left of a ring that a Native American shaman had put on his finger years before. He said that when I spoke about the satanic bondage of these things, it exploded into three pieces and fell from his finger onto the floor. After the ring exploded, he bolted for the altar to completely surrender his life to God.

Gordy thanked God for the deliverance of a curse he didn't even know was there until the ring came off. I still have the ring fragments he gave me that evening as a reminder of the awesome power of God.

I only knew Gordy for two months. Our friendship abruptly ended when he died suddenly of a heart attack. His funeral was like his wedding, surrounded by Harleys, but this time I was honored to officiate. During and after the service, all I could think about was how blessed he was to have accepted Christ as his personal Savior before his death.

In the two short months after his conversion, Gordy did a lot of good things, but the most significant was to take responsibility for his relationship with his girlfriend and child. He married and gave that little boy a name. Just like Jesus did when Gordy accepted Him as his Savior—He gave Gordy the name Christian.

Yet to all who received him, to those who believed in his name, he gave the right to become children of God—

children born not of natural descent, nor of human decision or a husband's will, but born of God.

JOHN 1:12,13

Former Vietnam veteran Chuck Dean surrendered his life to the Lord Jesus in 1986. He wanted to see other Vietnam vets seek spiritual change by surrendering their lives to God. In 1987 he became the international director of Point Man International Ministries, a veterans support organization. Chuck is the author of several books, including Nam Vet: Making Peace with Your Past.

55

THE CHECK'S IN THE MAIL
by Gena Bradford

*T*hirty-one years ago, at age nineteen and 1,500 miles away from home, I received a phone call that my father had suffered a major heart attack and wasn't expected to live through the night. It was my father's seventh heart attack.

At that time I had been estranged from my father and stepmother. Many years of hurt and anger separated us. I also knew that my dad did not have a personal relationship with Jesus and might die without ever understanding His plan of salvation.

I dropped to my knees in my college dorm, held onto the bed frame, and wept for my father. I cried and prayed for his salvation. I prayed that Jesus would save him from the destruction of alcoholism so he would know His great and wonderful love. I prayed that I might walk with my dad in paradise.

I cried out for the Lord's mercy. I asked for my father's salvation as part of my inheritance in Christ. After much intercession I rose to my feet and knew that I must get to the Oakland Army Hospital. I knew I had to talk to my dad.

I didn't have the money for an airline ticket and had no idea how I could get to California. I called the airlines to find out the price of a ticket. It was $107 to San Francisco.

I went to my mailbox that same morning and found a letter from my old friend, Pete. We had been corresponding since he had gone to the war in Vietnam and was writing to me from the trenches. Sometimes it took weeks to get a letter through the system.

I couldn't believe my eyes. In the envelope was a check for $107 and a scrawled note saying, "I don't know why I'm sending this except to say that I have a feeling that you needed this amount of money." I cried for joy.

I flew out the next day, not knowing whether or not my dad was still alive. I bumped into my uncle in the baggage claim area at the airport. He had just arrived from another city and drove me to Oakland to see my dad.

When I entered the hospital room where my dad had been sleeping, he looked up at me and smiled. Tears rolled down his cheeks. "Honey," he cried, "Jesus came to visit me yesterday. He stood by my bed and told me that He was going to heal me and give me the ability to love." Together we cried and rejoiced in the Lord's mercy and goodness.

Dad lived seven more years, and we developed a loving relationship. His health improved and he returned to work. God delivered him from alcoholism. My father became a man of prayer, and I finally felt loved by him.

I bumped into Pete at my 25-year high school reunion. Although he didn't remember his kindness, his obedience changed my life.

> *"If you believe, you will receive whatever you ask for in prayer."*
>
> MATTHEW 21:22

Gena Bradford enjoys her profession as a public school teacher. She is also a gifted singer/songwriter and freelance writer who has been published in various publications, including "Guideposts" magazine. Gena and her husband, Jack, live in Spokane, Washington, and have four grown children.

56

HEALED OF HIV
by John Shepherd

My story begins several years ago. I was burned-out and emotionally, mentally, and spiritually depressed. I regularly sold drugs to feed my own drug addiction. When I tested positive for HIV, I lost all hope and became consumed with fear.

I grew up in an environment of fear, anger, and torment. Living in a rough neighborhood filled me with great trepidation. I had no father, and my mother was a bitter, angry woman. I hated life.

By age thirteen I ran away from home and was living on the streets. I heavily used drugs, using needles, marijuana, LSD, and anything else I could find. The narcotics covered my fears and numbed my pain. When I was sixteen, my desperately hurting mother died from a prescription medication overdose.

I married at twenty and soon had a son. However, because our lives were consumed with drugs, we allowed our son to be adopted when he was three years old. My marriage dissolved at the same time, and I saw my life as a complete failure.

Knowing I needed help, I sought counseling. Hoping something good could come out of my life, I was determined to face my issues. I had bought $10,000 of music equipment and planned to return to school. It was then that I received the shocking news that I was HIV positive. For the first time in my life, I'd tried to turn my life around; but as soon as I did, I was given a death sentence.

Losing all hope, my drug use and depression grew. I started to move large quantities of drugs into Seattle. Why not? I would die soon anyway.

After a heavy drug binge one night, I overdosed. Total darkness surrounded me; I could physically feel the blackness, yet I didn't have a body. I experienced all of my past emotional pain at one time. I cried out weeping, "God, I don't want to come back to this life!" I hated life and everything about it.

Then Jesus appeared to me. We sat at a table and reviewed my past. I knew that if I wanted a second try at life, He would be with me. I sank back into my body and began gasping for air. Fear seized me as I realized that I had died and come back to life. I was emotionally and spiritually broken.

I still faced HIV, emotional pain, and bondage to drugs. My near-death experience didn't seem to help turn my life around. I was now living in a trailer and continued using dope. One day I was trying to inject a powerful drug into my arm when I heard a knock at the door. A policeman wanted me to move the trailer. When he saw the needle, he immediately escorted me to jail.

"Look God, You won't let me live, You won't let me die. I have to give You my life!" I cried behind bars. I fasted, prayed, and began to meditate on Scripture. I repented from my sinful lifestyle and asked God, "Please heal me and deliver me from the drugs." God answered my plea.

While attending Christian meetings in jail, the minister gave me Scriptures to think about while I was in my cell. After reading and rereading those Scriptures, I realized that because I was now in Christ, I was a new person. The old me had passed away, and I was a new creation. The revelation of my new identity brought God's power into that jail cell and broke my depression. Overwhelming peace and joy permeated me from top to bottom. All of the hurt and pain of my past left that instant! I also knew that God would heal me of AIDS.

Three months later I was released from jail and put on probation. I met Pastor Ed Allen, who had ministered to me while I was incarcerated. He generously allowed me to stay at his home. When Pastor Ed prayed for me, we both believed that I was healed.

Convinced that God healed me, I decided to get another AIDS test. I told the doctor, "God has done a miracle in my life, and I'm healed of HIV." She looked at me in disbelief.

When I returned to the office to hear the verdict, the doctor sat down next to me. "Either you have a guardian angel or God is really looking out for you," she said. "There's no trace of HIV in your system. None!"

I had been a broken man with no hope for the future, waiting to die. I was bound by the devil and bound by drug addiction, depression, and insanity. When I cried out to the Lord, He broke the chains that held me in bondage. He set me free and gave me a new life. I am healed and give God all the glory.

But now that you have been set free from sin and have become slaves to God, the benefit you reap leads to holiness, and the result is eternal life.

ROMANS 6:22

John Shepherd lives in the mountains of Cherith, Washington. After being gloriously set free from HIV in 1997, he continues to grow in his walk with the Lord Jesus Christ.

57

HE MEETS MY EVERY NEED
by Jack Bradford

*M*y wife and I were a young married couple with a new baby when I became unemployed. After three months of no income, I became increasingly depressed. Every job lead turned into a closed door. It was now December and we had drained our savings account. My wife wasn't working because she was at home with our child. We had no family or relatives nearby to call for help, and the bills were due.

Worry had turned me into a joyless, irritable man. When my wife made suggestions about jobs that I could apply for, I felt as though she was criticizing me. As a result, I rarely spoke to her. Feeling like a failure, I fearfully withdrew in my misery. I obsessively wondered, *How will I provide for my family?*

I finally cried out to the Lord about my need. There, in that quiet time of helplessness, I heard words call out from my memory like fresh fruit preserves from the pantry. "Behold the fowls of the air: for they sow not, neither do they reap, nor gather into barns; yet your heavenly Father feedeth them...Consider the lilies of the field, how they grow; they toil not, neither do they spin..." (Matt. 6:26,28 KJV). That's when I decided that my worrying was driving my wife and me crazy and produced nothing but anger and frustration.

I said, "Lord, I believe You love me and that You will provide for me. I'm going to change my attitude about my time off. I'll look at it as a vacation and enjoy every day until You lead me to a job. I realize I'm not alone, and I'm not on my own."

My wife and I counted our money, a mere three dollars. I walked to the store to buy milk and bread, the only food we could afford. I didn't know where we would get more money when that ran out, yet I knew my life was in God's hands.

I walked across a vacant field to get to the store. Other than dead weeds, it was barren. Halfway across the field I noticed something blowing in front of me. It looked like money! There on the ground was a five-dollar bill, some ones, and a ten. Picking them up I counted twenty dollars.

How could this be possible? I thought. I looked around to see where it came from or to whom it might belong, but no one was in sight. Seeing no houses, cars, or people, I was dumbfounded.

"My God, did You provide this?" I prayed. "This is a miracle! Won't my wife be surprised when I bring home meat and eggs?"

With a huge grin on my face I spent the money and carried the groceries home. We rejoiced and laughed at the unusual way God provided for us.

I had been home for an hour when we heard a knock. We opened the door to find our neighbor holding two bags of groceries. "I'm going on a long vacation and needed to clean out the refrigerator," she said as she handed us the food. We looked at each other in shock and giggled.

At dinnertime the same day, our landlord arrived. We were afraid to tell him that we didn't have the rent money. Before we could explain, he handed us a Christmas card and said, "Open it!"

He smiled as we read, "Merry Christmas. This card is good for one month of free rent." Our joy soared, and our faith skyrocketed.

I was determined to try again on my job search. Early the next morning I headed out to find new places to put in applications. As I drove down Division Street, I said, "Lord, where should I go?"

I felt impressed to turn right at the intersection and saw an employment agency that I hadn't yet tried. I parked the car and went inside. They assigned me to an employment counselor who turned out to be a college friend that I had not seen in three years. After our surprise meeting, I shared my dilemma.

He was very sympathetic. I was overeducated for some jobs, and there weren't any openings for the jobs that I was qualified for. I told him where I had looked and how the doors had slammed shut.

He picked up the phone and arranged an interview for a state job. They hired me that same week, and I have worked for the state for over 30 years. I soon plan to retire.

There has never been another time that our family has not received the provision that God promised in His Word.

And my God shall meet all of your needs according to His glorious riches in Christ Jesus.

PHILIPPIANS 4:19

Jack Bradford has been married for 35 years and is a father of four children. He is a counselor for the state of Washington and has a seminary degree in pastoral counseling and a masters degree from Whitworth College in Spokane, Washington.

58

EVEN THE DEMONS BOW
by Reverend Lorelei Wilcox

In 1999 I preached at a village in Punjab, India, prior to an evening crusade. About 200 people attended the meeting. After sharing a message from the Word of God, I began to pray for the people.

One man, Mr. Singh, came forward for prayer. When I laid my hands on him and began to pray, I was led to cast out a dumb spirit. "You dumb spirit, come out of him in the name of Jesus," I commanded. Although I didn't know it at the time, Mr. Singh was mute from birth and had never spoken. After I rebuked the spirit, Mr. Singh began to speak immediately.

I continued to pray for others in the healing line when I noticed a commotion by Mr. Singh. He became pale and his eyes rolled back in his head. For over five minutes, nobody could detect a pulse in him. Some men had gathered around him and held him up by his arms.

I was again led to cast demons out of him. As I began to pray, I saw in the spiritual realm the image of a white angel who appeared to be over seven feet tall standing behind him. When I cast out the remaining demons, his coloring returned and his eyes opened.

That night Mr. Singh shared his testimony. He said that when I prayed for him, he lost his memory as complete darkness covered his eyes. He knew that he had died. When God brought him back to life, he opened his eyes and was surprised to hear himself speak for the first time in his life.

Mr. Singh was completely set free from demonic possession and is now an associate pastor at a church in Punjub, India.

... "You deaf and mute spirit," he [Jesus] said, "I command you, come out of him and never enter him again."

The spirit shrieked, convulsed him violently and came out. The boy looked so much like a corpse that many said, "He's dead."

But Jesus took him by the hand and lifted him to his feet, and he stood up.

MARK 9:25-27

Lorelei Wilcox teaches and preaches the Word of God throughout the world with signs, wonders, and miracles. She is the founder and president of Lord of the Nations Training Center and oversees House of the Lord Ministries with her husband, Jay.

59

BEN'S GIFT

by Pastor Rick Sharkey

*T*wenty years ago our family was blessed with a baby boy. Ben was the joy and the center of attention of our family of five. His two older sisters adored him and scrambled to his every possible want. We were equally smitten with our "man child."

When Ben was six months old, he developed a fever and became listless. We suspected he was developing a cold. Having raised two other children, his symptoms did not alarm us nor cause us reason to panic. We took Ben to the doctor, and he was prescribed with a mild medication.

The next morning Ben developed a rash over his tiny body. We still didn't feel there was a need for great concern. We continued to give him the medicine and comforted him in every way we could, offering short prayers for his healing.

Over the next few days, Ben's condition continued to worsen. The rash developed into blotches, and some spots began to darken and appeared like bruises.

We were now concerned and returned to our doctor. He tactfully said, "I don't want to alarm you, but this could be something serious. It looks like symptoms of leukemia." He made arrangements for blood tests to be taken the next day.

We returned home with a black cloud hanging over our lives. We could have fallen apart or abandoned our faith, but God is bigger than disease, bad reports, and life-gripping fear.

We took out our Bible, found Scriptures for healing, and said to the mountain of infirmity and to the fear, "It is written, '...with His stripes we are healed'" (Isa. 53:5 KJV). Although we didn't see anything different, we had an assurance that Ben would be healed.

That night Ben was restless and uncomfortable and began crying in the middle of the night. I was restless as well and picked him up and rocked him.

Putting Ben on my chest, I cradled his head on my shoulder and began to talk to the Lord about him. As I prayed, a song rose up in my heart about God's mercy. The lyrics and melody spilled out. "The mercy of the Lord endures and lasts forever. It crosses mighty oceans and soars on wings of eagles. It enters the depths of darkness and bursts out on beams of lightning. Oh yes, that's the mercy of the Lord."

God's Presence filled the room as I sung, and joy and love enveloped us. As I continued to sing, Ben's temperature began to decrease and peace rested on him.

I knew the battle had been won. Whether Ben had contracted leukemia or some other illness, my son was healed. I took Ben back to his bed, and he slept soundly the rest of the night.

We took Ben in for testing the next day, although I already knew in my heart what the outcome would be. The blotches and the spots began to diminish and in a matter of days were gone. The laboratory tests didn't show any signs of any abnormalities or infection.

Our doctor said, "I know what I saw on Ben, and I know that something has changed."

Today Ben is a strong, twenty-year-old man who is in pursuit of God's heart. He also has a gift of music. I believe this came into his life on the same night God healed his body.

This is the confidence we have...if we ask anything according to His will, he hears us.

And if we know that he hears us—whatever we ask—we know that we have what we asked of him.

1 JOHN 5:14,15

Rick Sharkey is senior pastor and founder of Spokane Christian Center and Academy, located in Spokane, Washington. He and his lovely wife, Linda, have been married 29 years and have three children.

60

THERAPY FROM HEAVEN

by Sheila Honnold

My husband and I were high school sweethearts and enjoy a great marriage. Our relationship throughout our marriage has been strong, and we rarely faced conflict. There was one area in our marriage, however, that was not the way I felt it was supposed to be.

My desire for sex had completely diminished after having children. Considering my sex drive was not strong to begin with, this further decrease was troubling to our marital relationship. Raising children and fulfilling multiple responsibilities as a mother and a homemaker left me with little to give to my husband at the end of the day.

Unable to deny the problem, I shared my feelings with him. I felt, however, I had to fulfill my wifely "duty" and not withhold sex from him. Sexual intercourse became something I dreaded. I hated it and felt used, hurt, frustrated, and angry. God intended sex to be lovely and fulfilling, but for me it had become something dreadful.

Several years passed while my sexual thorn in the flesh continued to worsen. Knowing how unhappy my husband was about my aversion to sex only added to my despair.

After being physically distant from him for four years, I heard about a guest speaker who was scheduled to visit our church. Knowing he was spiritually gifted in the arena of healing, I wanted to attend the service. I did not expect to be ministered to at the service but simply felt the need to be at church.

When I suggested that we go to church that night, my husband made it clear that he did not want to go and was obviously grumpy about my suggestion to attend. I knew by his negative response that I should drop the matter.

Knowing that prayer was my only hope, I asked God to put it on his heart to allow me to attend the service. God quickly answered my prayer. My husband willingly offered to watch the kids and suggested I attend the service by myself.

After the speaker shared a powerful message, he began to pray for various needs. I was surprised when he said, "There are some couples here that need their relationship restored, and they should come forward for prayer right now." No one responded.

He repeated, "I know there are couples here needing restoration in their relationship. I'd like you to come up now." Again no one responded.

I thought, *I'd be up there in a heartbeat if he hadn't said "couple."* Because my husband was not with me, I didn't feel the man was talking to me.

The speaker said he was going to wait until someone came forward. He waited and waited. Finally he said, "There is someone here by him or herself that needs prayer in this area."

I knew that he was speaking to me and quickly went forward for prayer. Although I didn't know if the minister knew exactly what area he should pray for, I surely did.

I had prayed for years for my sex drive to change. That evening God instantly changed me. Years of therapy could not have accomplished what God did that night. Our sexual relationship was instantly transformed. Instead of dreading sex once a month, we now freely enjoy it on a regular basis.

Now to each one the manifestation of the Spirit is given for the common good.

To one there is given through the Spirit the message of wisdom, to another the message of knowledge by means of the same Spirit.

1 CORINTHIANS 12:7,8

Sheila Honnold and her husband are happier today than when they first married. She left her Consumer Sales career to raise their three children, now ages 13, 11, and 7. Sheila and her husband are avid snow ski enthusiasts.

61

MIRACLE ON STEVENS PASS
by Dave Wagner

$\mathcal{O}$n the evening of October 17, 1999, my wife and I were returning from a day trip in Seattle. As we were coming through Stevens Pass, we encountered the first snow of the winter. The road didn't look like it was particularly slippery, just wet.

As I entered a right-hand curve, I began sliding across the road into the left lane. I eased off the gas, but the car continued at the same speed. I tried steering back into my lane to no avail. The car kept sliding toward a section of guardrail at the end of a bridge.

Halfway across the bridge, a snowplow was heading toward us. I thought we were "toast." My wife was sitting in the passenger seat and began to repeat the name of Jesus over and over. All she could see was the blade of the snowplow getting closer.

Just as we were about to hit the guardrail, our car quit sliding and shot onto the bridge. At the same instant, the snowplow had cleared the snow from the end of the bridge. This gave us just enough space to squeeze between the blade of the snowplow and the end of the bridge.

A car was approaching from the far end of the bridge, so I tried to steer into the right lane but still didn't have any control of the car. I could not speed up, slow down, or steer. Much to my amazement, our car maneuvered itself into the right lane and went across the bridge as if I was driving.

We later talked with the driver of the snowplow. He had been involved in an accident on the bridge the year before. He explained that when a snowplow and a car meet head-on, the occupants of the car are killed every time.

"I knew your car was out of control when I saw you sliding across the road," he told my wife. "I was waiting to see if you were going to be able to regain control before I changed lanes, hoping we might prevent a head-on collision. I waited until the last possible instant then moved into the left lane. I expected you to hit the guardrail and then bounce off of it and into my blade."

The driver told my wife that I had done a great job of driving. He couldn't believe I was able to regain control and then steer our car between the plow and the bridge without losing control again.

"It wasn't my husband driving," she explained. "The Lord was in control the whole time."

I'm sure that when my wife called on the name of Jesus, He sent angels to protect us. I still wonder if any of them were bruised when they got between our car and the guardrail. God promised to never leave us nor forsake us, not even on a lonely, dark highway in the middle of a snowstorm.

...I will be with you; I will never leave you nor forsake you.

JOSHUA 1:5

David Wagner is a semiretired mechanical engineer living in Leavenworth, Washington, with his wife, Laura. David accepted Jesus as Lord at age thirty-one. His hobbies include steam-powered logging and modeling history. He is the editor of "Safety Valve Letters" for his local newspaper.

62

CONCEIVED BY GRACE

by Diane White

*E*ver since I can remember, I had always wanted six children. After falling in love with a wheat farmer, we married and moved onto the farm. It seemed the perfect place to raise a large family.

After two years of marriage, Dave and I decided it was time to start our family. We were ecstatic to learn that our first attempt to become pregnant was a success. The pregnancy, however, only lasted a short time. Alarmed when I started to spot blood, we knew something was seriously wrong; and the loss of our first baby was devastating to both of us.

Several months after my miscarriage, I still didn't feel well. Two weeks before Christmas I started to experience severe cramping in my lower abdomen. I saw my doctor, but he was unable to determine what was wrong. The discomfort continued at an increasing rate, but because I thought the pain must be in my head, I didn't go back to the doctor.

I had planned to sing several solos in the upcoming church Christmas musical. I was losing weight and felt horrible, and it became clear that I could not participate in the program. The night before the musical, I was curled up in a fetal position in my bed in an attempt to endure the abdominal pain. I had difficulty breathing and by morning I couldn't walk.

David went to church the next day without me. When my mom called that afternoon to ask how I was feeling, I told her I couldn't get off the couch. She insisted that I call the doctor. Although he was heading to Spokane, he agreed to see me.

After examining me, he instructed us to go directly to the hospital in Spokane. We headed out in the midst of a blinding snowstorm.

At the hospital we learned that I had a tubal pregnancy. My fallopian tube was bursting, and I was bleeding internally. My difficulty in breathing was caused by blood collecting in my esophagus. After undergoing emergency surgery, I learned that I had been over three months pregnant. Because the baby was the size of a chicken egg and fallopian tubes are only tiny, narrow tubes, it was a serious matter.

As a result of the tubal pregnancy, I lost my right fallopian tube. I was devastated to learn that I had lost twins; one miscarried and the other fetus was stuck in the fallopian tube. This news grieved me because I had always dreamed of having twins.

After several years of unsuccessfully conceiving, doctors proceeded with tests to determine why I was unable to become pregnant. One of the tests involved the scraping of my uterine lining. By scraping the lining, the doctor could evaluate whether or not the uterus was able to carry a pregnancy.

I was told that the procedure had to be performed close to my menstrual cycle in order to avoid the risk of aborting a possible pregnancy. To ensure that women were not pregnant, doctors routinely order pregnancy tests before the scraping procedure.

Before beginning the 60-mile trip to Spokane, I was supposed to take ibuprofen to minimize the pain that normally follows the test. I didn't take any medication because I sensed in my spirit that I might be pregnant.

Throughout my infertility problems, I claimed God's promises and read the stories of Hannah and Rachel. God opened their wombs and blessed them. I knew He would do the same for me. I was confident that God was going to bless Dave and me with children.

When we arrived at the doctor's office, my pregnancy test turned out negative. The negative result surprised me because of what I sensed in my heart. The doctor then proceeded with the test.

After the doctor scraped the inside of my uterus, he said he needed more tissue and had to scrape a second time. After the second uterine scraping, he offered me drugs for the pain. I still didn't feel peace about taking any type of pain medication, so I passed on his offer. Back home, I suffered the normal cramping and spotting from the scraping.

Two weeks after the procedure, I was concerned because I still hadn't started my menstrual cycle. After contacting the doctor, he asked me to come to his office right away. After an exam and pregnancy test, I learned that I was six weeks pregnant!

The Lord protected my son from the doctor's scalpel. I often tell Ethan Aaron that God has great plans for him because his life was miraculously spared before he was born.

God has continued to bless David and me with four more children. Even though we suffered the loss of the miscarriage and tubal pregnancy, we are now a family of seven.

> *So in the course of time Hannah conceived and gave birth to a son. She named her son Samuel, saying, "Because I asked the Lord for him."*
>
> 1 SAMUEL 1:20

Diane White and her husband, David, are wheat farmers in eastern Washington. They have five beautiful children. Diane has a beautiful voice and often enjoys singing in her church.

63

IN HIS HAND
by Colleen Johnson

$\mathscr{I}$ wasn't raised in a Christian home. The only time the name of God and Jesus Christ were mentioned in our house was when somebody was swearing. Like many households, although our parents often spoke the forbidden words, my siblings and I got our mouths washed out with soap if we ever uttered them.

Susie and Mimi Evans, my neighbors from across the street, were my first exposure to God. "If you don't believe that Jesus is God's Son, then when God throws fireballs upon the earth to burn it up, you'll burn up with it," they told me. "Then you'll burn in hell for the rest of your life." Needless to say, I quickly confessed Jesus as my Lord and Savior right then and there. I didn't want to burn in hell!

Susie and Mimi Evans took me to their Catholic church from time to time. Watching the nuns in their traditional habits and seeing the priests perform religious ceremonies sparked my curiosity about a God that appeared unreachable to me. I was certain that priests and nuns were the only ones who could talk to Him.

When I was a young teen, our family of seven outgrew the small house we had lived in since I was four. My parents sold our home, and we lived in a rented house for a while. However, they wanted us to start school in the area they planned to buy their next house. So every day my mom drove us across town, dropping my younger brother off at the grade school and then my older brother and me at the junior high.

Back in the sixties, station wagons were the normal mode of transportation for many families, and we were no exception. The front passenger door of our station wagon didn't work very well and seat belts were not used at that time. Because the front passenger door was difficult to shut, it took a great deal of force to make sure that it was closed. Once several "slams" were made to secure the door, we never sat too close to it because it occasionally opened when we least expected it.

To open the door, a forceful push had to be applied once again. With as much strength as we could muster, we'd thrust our shoulder up against the door, hoping to open it on the first try.

One day after my mother picked me up from school, we headed across town to go home. On this particular day, only Mom and I were in the car. The family dog was sitting on my lap. I wasn't sitting particularly close to the car door because I knew it could fly open.

After stopping at a red light at a major intersection in town, the light turned green. When Mom accelerated to make a left-hand turn, my door flew open, and I was thrown from the car. I yelled, "Oh, God!"

Although I don't remember if my eyes were open or closed, everything turned dark. In the darkness, I saw an incredibly huge hand scoop me up and turn me over.

I found myself sitting on the pavement. The dog had fallen out of the car with me and was stumbling to get its balance. I didn't feel myself fall out of the car nor did I feel myself land on the ground.

As I came to my senses, I thought about the fact that I was wearing a skirt. I felt embarrassed, certain that it must have come up and given bystanders full view of my undergarments.

Glancing down at my skirt, I found it perfectly tucked underneath me as if I were sitting on a chair. I wasn't hurt in any way. Not even a scratch!

My mother pulled the car over while others who witnessed the ordeal stopped to help. My mother was panic-stricken and scanned my body for injuries. Everyone was in awe that I didn't suffer any injuries.

After Mom and caring strangers made sure I was all right, they put my dog and me back in the car. The door was secured once again, and we completed our journey home.

Returning home, I went to my room. I stood looking out the window for some time, wondering what had just happened to me. I knew God had a plan for my life.

though he stumble, he will not fall, for the Lord upholds him with his hand.

PSALM 37:24

Colleen Johnson was in her late 20s when she began to look for the answers to life. God delivered her from depression, suicide, and alcoholism. Colleen says, "The most amazing thing of all is that with all my shortcomings, God still loved me." She was born and raised in Spokane, Washington, where she currently manages an apartment complex. She has a son and two daughters.

64

THE HEAVENS ROLLED BACK

by David F. Winecoff

My father had a weekly routine of going to church every Sunday. Although I experienced rough times during my childhood, this routine was a comfort to me. Through Dad's example, I gained a reverence for God that influenced me to stay on the straight and narrow instead of living a wild, raucous life.

The truths I learned each Sunday morning kept me going throughout the week. However, I didn't feel as though I was influencing other people in the way that I wanted to. In an effort to change my impact, I read many self-help books seeking guidance.

Later in life, I was married with four children when I made a near-disastrous financial mistake. My wife and I sold our home in Virginia and bought a new home near Seattle. We moved to be closer to our parents and hoped that I would get an assignment in Washington. Unfortunately, the sale of our home in Virginia fell through, and for nine months we made double house payments, which almost caused us to declare bankruptcy.

I set several personal goals during that time. One of which was to read the Bible. I felt that I lacked the personal charisma I saw in other Christians. I was a church member, but Bible reading was not a daily habit; and I wanted to give it a try. I took my roles as husband, father, and marine officer seriously but needed more wisdom.

Seven months later, I had made progress in all of the goals that I had set except for the goals regarding my spiritual life. "Ten minutes a night!" I declared and placed my unused Bible next to my bed. I started in the New Testament and began my nightly reading. The first ten days were merely a discipline.

On the eleventh day, when I read Matthew 3:11, my spirit leapt at the words, "...He will baptize you with the Holy Spirit and with fire." This quickening was a new experience for me. Charged with a renewed motivation to study the Bible, I continued; and much to my delight, this nightly routine became enjoyable!

As I was reading the book of Luke, my spirit again leapt. *What is this quickening?* I wondered. It happened again when I read "...'You must be born again'" (John 3:7).

I had grown up going to church every Sunday morning. Although I prayed and felt that I had a personal relationship with Jesus, this quickening was a new experience. I kept reading and sensed that something was happening. I again read "...He will baptize you with the Holy Spirit and with fire." In a highly unusual posture for a marine, I raised my arms in surrender and said: "Jesus, I want what You're promising here. I want to be baptized with the Holy Spirit."

The far corner of my room instantly rolled back like a veil drawn open. I peered into heaven and saw Jesus interceding in prayer. I watched in awe as He became outlined with many colors of light, streams of glory it seemed. Jesus never spoke a word but twice nodded at me.

My spirit felt as if a river flowed through my body, cleansing my innermost being. I could not speak and fell to the floor. When I attempted to lift to my knees, the veil closed.

The stars were ablaze in the sky as I walked outside. Feeling a thousand feet tall, I was alive in a way that I had never experienced. This exuberant joy stayed with me through that night and the next day.

I received an unexpected call the next day. The house in Virginia had sold and would close in three weeks. The full sale price recouped all our financial losses.

A second unsolicited call came from HQs, Marine Corps, who asked if I was interested in becoming a marine officer instructor at the University of Washington. I had acquired my master's degree for this position, but a later change in seniority requirements had put it beyond my reach. HQMC waived the new rules to give me this job.

Later that same day I was prompted to turn to Psalm 104. "He wraps himself in light as with a garment; he stretches out the heavens like a tent and lays the beams of his upper chambers on their waters..." (vv. 2,3). After reading this verse, I felt that my vision was confirmed.

"Lord, why would You manifest Yourself to me and not to the world?" I asked.

He answered me through His Word, "...If a man love me, he will keep my words: and my Father will love him, and we will come unto him, and make our abode with him" (John 14:23 KJV).

This vision gave me a new understanding of the power available to me as a Spirit-filled believer. It clearly showed what I had been lacking and brought about a new level of joy in everything I do. I have gained a greater degree of knowledge in understanding events and enduring trials that would have otherwise broken me. And finally, I'm impacting the lives of others in a way that was not possible before this wonderful revelation.

The Spirit-filled life is a wonderful adventure. I knew God loved me before but had no idea that such a thin veil separated us from Jesus.

> *"But you will receive power when the Holy Spirit comes on you; and you will be my witnesses in Jerusalem, and in all Judea and Samaria, and to the ends of the earth."*

ACTS 1:8

David Winecoff is a retired marine, husband, father, grandfather, writer, teacher, and rancher. He is the author of Secret Weapon: Men Overcoming Chaos. *Additional works by him include* The Coming Ambush *(based on the book of Revelations) and* Hidden Wars: A Believer's Battle Against Familiar Spirits.

65

HEALING IS MINE!
by Tom Marszalek

*A*s an adult I had become accustomed to neck and back pain and eventually accepted and expected it to be a normal part of middle-aged life. Because I felt that I had no other choice, I learned to live with the constant physical discomfort.

By 1990, however, the pain resonating from my neck became so intense that I often walked around with my arm lifted up over my head in an effort to find temporary relief. I'm sure this caused some people to look at me with upraised eyebrows, but I didn't care. And being the "tough" man that I am, I avoided medical attention until I couldn't stand the pain any longer.

I saw a chiropractor and was quickly diagnosed with a degenerative disk disease. The doctor said it was probably caused by a previous neck injury. *Could it have been the result of a helicopter crash in Vietnam?* I wondered. *Or maybe I hurt my neck while playing pond hockey with the guys in my younger days?* Although I was unable to identify the source of the injury, I knew one thing was for sure: I hurt!

After several months of visiting the "bone bender" three times a week, I improved slightly. I was either getting better, or I had grown more tolerant to the pain. I started to rejoice in the improvement but quickly realized my joy was premature.

During a routine chiropractic adjustment, an excruciating pain shot through my neck and down my left arm. Unfortunately, this pain became the norm from that day forward.

At that time my wife, Therese, and I were actively involved in a small, close-knit church. Mere infants in our walk with the Lord, we were just beginning to understand that God sent His Son to die for our sins. When I first read in the Bible that Jesus also took our sicknesses and diseases upon Himself while hanging on the cross, I thought, *Supernatural healing is only for the guy who has been a Christian for a long time and knows how to get that blessing from God!*

When the pain again became unbearable, I sought the advice of a neurosurgeon who promptly scheduled me for surgery to fuse the vertebrae in my neck. Afterward, the surgery was considered a success, that is, if you consider a 75 percent reduction in pain a success. However, I did survive most days without raiding the medicine cabinet for anti-inflammatory medications. I cruised through several years of "managing" the pain by trying to minimize any heavy lifting. But a guy's got to do what a guy's got to do, right?

In the fall of 2001, I developed severe pain in my lower back. Every morning I struggled to get out of bed and could barely lift my leg high enough to put my pants on. One day while shopping at a local store, I bent down to get a product from a lower shelf and couldn't stand up. Humiliated, I dropped to the floor and had to wait until a kind customer helped me to my feet.

I contacted a Christian chiropractor, thinking that somehow he would have a better chance of success than other doctors. I began rigorous adjustments three times a week only to discover that my pain worsened with each passing day.

After several months of treatments, the doctor acknowledged that I was going downhill and recommended that I also begin physical therapy three times a week to supplement the adjustments to my back. I was now looking at six appointments each week just to help me get my pants on! The doctor's appointments were not only using up all of my spare time, but they were also draining my bank account. Discouragement set in.

A few days after scheduling my first series of physical therapy sessions, I was praying while driving to an out-of-state business appointment. Frustrated, I asked God the proverbial question, "Why me?"

Waiting silently for a response, Bible verses that I had studied for over ten years began to come to my mind. *Jesus took the infirmities of mankind while He was on the cross,* I thought. *That includes all of the pain I have in my back! By His stripes, I am healed.*

In the past I had prayed for many people to be healed and had voiced the same words that God was now reminding me of. *Do I really believe His Word?* I asked myself.

Yes, I do! God's Word is true, and I believe every word of it! Healing is mine!

As I continued to drive, I confessed my unwavering belief and trust in God's Word. I demanded that the endless back pain that I had suffered from for so long bow to the name of Jesus! He bore my infirmities and took my pain, so I don't need to experience any more pain. That day, I decided to receive my healing and put up a "no trespassing" sign on my body. What I had previously believed with my intellect, I now knew in my heart.

I couldn't wait to get home and tell Therese that my back was healed. I was so excited that I could have run the entire 150 miles.

When I walked through the door, Therese grinned. "You're walking different!" she said. "What's happened to you?"

"I received my healing today!" I testified.

I cancelled the physical therapy appointments and never saw the chiropractor again.

This was in March of 2002. The following Sunday after my road trip, our church had a special guest speaker by the name of Bob Lemon. After he had finished preaching, he began to minister to the congregation.

He was ministering to people in the back of the church when he stopped and said, "Someone is being healed of pain in their lower back right now. You are feeling heat where you previously had experienced severe pain. You're healed. Receive your healing right now!"

When he said this, it felt as though God had put a heating pad on my lower back.

"Whoever has been healed of lower back pain, raise your hand," he said.

As the heat continued to radiate throughout my lower back, my hands immediately shot up, proclaiming victory and giving God the glory! I believed this word confirmed my healing.

I have enjoyed a pain-free life ever since. God's Word is true. He is still on the throne and wants us to use the power and authority that has been entrusted to us through His Son Jesus Christ!

I pray also that the eyes of your heart may be enlightened in order that you may know the hope to which he has called you, the riches of his glorious inheritance in the saints.

EPHESIANS 1:18

Tom Marszalek has worked in the industrial automation market for the past 25 years. He enjoys playing guitar and camping with his family. Tom lives in Spokane, Washington, with his wife and three children. He also has two grown children in Seattle.

66

GOD'S GOT YOUR NUMBER
by Ken Gaub

God, sometimes I wonder if You really know where I am! I thought. A melancholy cloud of self-pity enshrouded my mind. My hands tensed their grip on the steering wheel, and I stared through the windshield of our bus. The endless ribbon of super-highway stretched before me as I recalled the last few days of our fast-paced existence. I seemed to have used up all my faith in ministering to others. Even my sense of humor was hollow. *God, even a preacher needs to know that You are aware of him once in awhile,* I pleaded inside.

"Hey, Dad. Let's get some pizza." The voice of my younger son, Dan, stirred me out of my self-induced cocoon of despondency. My wife, Barbara, and daughter Becki agreed with Dan. It had been a long day, and it was way past time to eat.

"Okay," I yelled back. A large green sign loomed ahead. I flipped on my right turn signal and picked up the CB microphone to inform my oldest son, Nathan, of our plans to pull off the highway. He and his wife followed closely in another bus.

We exited from I-75 and turned onto Route 741 just south of Dayton, Ohio. Bright, colorful signs advertising a wide variety of fast food restaurants were a welcome sight. Satisfied murmurs arose behind me as we sighted the local pizza parlor.

As I maneuvered the big Silver Eagle bus into the parking lot, Dan and Becki were already clamoring to get out to go into the restaurant. Even examining menus offered a diversion from the limited activities available inside our "home on wheels."

Barbara stood at the bottom step and turned to wait for me. I sat staring into space. "Aren't you coming, Ken?" she asked.

"Naw, I'm not really hungry," I replied. "You go ahead with the kids. I need to stretch out and unwind a bit."

"Okay, we'll be back soon," her voice trailed off.

I moved back into the living room area to the sofa, folded my arms behind my head, leaned back, and sighed. *It really is a beautiful day,* I thought as I glanced out the window. *Maybe I should get some fresh air.*

I stepped outside, closed the bus doors, and looked around. Noticing a Dairy Queen down the street, I thought, *Maybe I'm thirsty.*

After purchasing a Coke, I strolled in the direction of the bus, still musing about my feelings of God's apathy toward me. The impatient ringing of a telephone somewhere up the street jarred me out of my doldrums. It was coming from a phone booth at a service station on the corner. As I approached, I heard the phone continuing its unanswered ring! Ring! Ring!

I paused and looked to see if anyone was going to answer the phone. Noise from the traffic flowing through the busy intersection must have drowned out the sound because the service station attendant continued looking after his customers, oblivious to the incessant ringing.

Why doesn't someone answer that phone? I wondered. The ringing continued. I began reasoning, *It may be important. What if it's an emergency?*

I started to walk away, but curiosity overcame my indifference. I stepped inside the booth and picked up the phone. "Hello," I said casually and took a big sip of Coke.

The operator whined, "Long distance call for Ken Gaub."

My eyes widened, and I almost choked on a chunk of ice from my Coke. Swallowing hard, I said, "You're crazy!" Realizing I shouldn't speak to an operator like that, I added, "This can't be! I was just walking down the street, not bothering anyone, and the phone was ringing...."

The operator ignored my crude explanation and asked once more, "Is Ken Gaub there? I have a long distance call for him."

It took a moment to gain control of my babblings, but I finally replied, "Yes, he is." Searching for a possible explanation, I suddenly had the answer. "I know what this is! I'm on candid camera!"

While trying to locate the hidden camera, I reached up and tried to smooth my hair. I wanted to look my best for all those millions of television viewers. Stepping outside the phone booth and looking quickly in every direction, the telephone cord nearly broke as I stretched it to its limit. I couldn't find a camera anywhere! Impatiently, the operator interrupted again.

"I have a long distance call for Ken Gaub, sir. Is he there?"

Still shaken, as well as perplexed, I asked, "How in the world can this be? How did you reach me here? I was walking down the street, not bothering anyone, the pay phone started ringing, and I decided to answer it." My voice grew louder in the excitement. "I just answered it on chance. You can't mean me. This is impossible!"

"Well," the operator asked, "is Mr. Gaub there or isn't he?" The tone of her voice convinced me the call was real and that her patience was at its limit.

I then replied, "Yes, he is. I'm he."

She was not convinced. "Are you sure?" she asked.

Flustered, I half-laughingly replied, "As far as I know, at this point I am."

To avoid any further disasters, I sat my Coke down as I heard another voice say, "Yes that's him, operator. I believe that's him!"

I listened dumbfounded to a strange voice identify herself. The caller blurted, "Ken Gaub, I'm Millie from Harrisburg, Pennsylvania. You don't know me, but I'm desperate. Please help me."

"What can I do for you?" I responded.

She began weeping. I waited until she gained control, and then she continued. "I'm about to commit suicide, and I just finished writing a note. While writing it, I began to pray and tell God I really didn't want to do this. I suddenly remembered seeing you on television and thought if I could just talk to you, you could help me. I know that was impossible because I didn't know how to reach you, and I didn't know anyone who could help me find you. I continued writing my suicide note because I could see no way out of my situation. As I wrote, numbers came to my mind, and I scribbled them down."

At this point she began weeping again, and I prayed silently for wisdom to help her.

She continued, "I looked at the numbers and thought, *Wouldn't it be wonderful if I had a miracle from God, and He has given me Ken's phone number?* I decided to try calling it. I figured it was worth the chance. It really was. I can't believe I'm talking to you. Are you in your office in California?"

I replied, "Lady, I don't have an office in California. My office is in Yakima, Washington."

Surprised, she asked, "Oh, really, then where are you?"

"Don't you know?" I responded. "You made the call."

She explained, "But I don't even know what area I'm calling. I just dialed the number that I had on this paper."

I told her, "Ma'am, you won't believe this, but I'm in a phone booth in Dayton, Ohio!"

"Really?" she exclaimed. "Well, what are you doing there?"

I kidded her gently. "Well, I'm answering the phone. It was ringing as I walked by, so I answered it."

Knowing this encounter could only have been arranged by God, I began to counsel the woman. As she told me of her despair and frustration, the Presence of the Holy Spirit flooded the phone booth giving me words of wisdom beyond my ability. In a matter of moments, she prayed the sinner's prayer and met the One who would lead her out of her situation into a new life.

I walked away from that telephone booth with an electrifying sense of our heavenly Father's concern for each of His children. I was astounded as I thought of the astronomical odds of this happening. With all the million of phones and innumerable combinations of numbers, only an all-knowing God could have caused that woman to call that number in that phone booth at that moment in time.

Forgetting my Coke and nearly bursting with exhilaration, I bounded up the steps and into the bus. I wondered if my family would believe my story. *Maybe I better not tell this,* I thought; but I couldn't contain it. "Barb, you won't believe this! God knows where I am!"

When you pass through the waters, I will be with you; and when you pass through the rivers, they will not sweep over

you. When you walk through the fire, you will not be burned;
the flames will not set you ablaze.

ISAIAH 43:2

Ken has been in ministry most of his adult life. He's traveled over 6 million miles to
over 100 foreign countries and has taken over 85 trips to Israel. His answers to
complex questions combined with his unusual experience and humor make him a
dynamic, sought after speaker all over the world. His books include God's Got Your
Number, Answers To Questions You Always Wanted To Ask, Dreams, Plans and
Goals, 20 Success Secrets to Sky High Faith *and* Rearranging Your Mental
Furniture. *His ministry office is based in Yakima, Washington.*

CONCLUSION

$\mathscr{O}$rdinary people have experienced the miracles you have just read; however, a divine Author performed these miracles. This Author is the same God who spoke the universe into existence. He is the same God who created humankind to love Him, to commune with Him, and to be called His children.

You have read about a handful of supernatural miracles that God is performing throughout the earth today; miracles that demonstrate His unfailing love, His everlasting mercy, and His desire to breathe hope into the hopeless. God has a miracle waiting for each person on earth—one that far exceeds the miracles that were shared in this book. Every individual has the opportunity to personally know the God of miracles through a relationship with Jesus Christ, the incarnate Son of God.

God created man to have a personal, intimate relationship with Him. He gave man dominion over the earth and wanted him to enjoy a life of abundant blessings both now and into eternity. That divine relationship was broken when sin entered the world through the disobedience of Adam. As a result of this sin, man had no hope of restoring his relationship to God because sin makes it impossible to be in the Presence of a holy God.

But God so loved us that He made a way for that relationship to be restored by sending His Son Jesus to die on the cross. Jesus paid the penalty for sin; He died and was raised to life. His shed blood on the cross is the only way for our relationship to be restored with God!

Although the priceless gift of forgiveness of sin and eternal life through Jesus is available, it is up to us to personally receive it. Jesus will not force Himself into our life. He comes into our heart and cleanses us from sin by invitation only.

Jesus is offering you the gift of life. If you haven't already done so, receive it and make Him Lord of your life. If you want to accept God's gift of forgiveness and eternal life, please pray this prayer:

> *Father, I come to You in the name of Jesus. I know I am a sinner and need Your forgiveness. I repent of my sins. I believe Jesus died on the cross and was raised from the dead so I can be free from sin and eternal death. I invite Him to come into my life. I confess with my mouth that Jesus is my Lord and Savior. Heavenly Father, fill me with Your Holy Spirit. I want to receive everything You have for my life. In Jesus' name, amen.*

If you have received Jesus as your Savior, you are now a child of the King of kings and Lord of lords! You are born again and all of heaven is rejoicing over your decision to follow Christ. (Luke 15:10.) God has removed your sins from you as far as the east is from the west. (Ps. 103:12.) The old you is now gone and the new you has taken its place. (2 Cor. 5:17.) You are a brand-new creation! The greatest miracle on earth has taken place—your salvation. To God be the glory!

To learn more about your new life in Christ, we suggest that you attend a church that teaches the full Word of God, read your Bible daily, and stay in communication through prayer with God every day.

If you have a supernatural miracle to share for consideration in subsequent *Miracles Still Happen* books or have experienced the miracle of the new birth by asking Jesus into your heart, please write us at *Miracles Still Happen,* P.O. Box 1754, Post Falls, Idaho 83877, or email us at incnarts@earthlink.net or kingskids5@comcast.net.

ENDNOTES

Foreword

[1] Based on a definition from *The Oxford English Dictionary, Volume VI, L-M* (London: Oxford University Press, Amen House, 1961), s.v. "**Miracle.**"

Introduction by Therese Marszalek

[1] "...Phrases similar to this [last days] occur frequently in the Scriptures. They do not imply that the world was soon coming to an end, but that that was the 'last' dispensation, the 'last' period of the world. There had been the patriarchal period, the period under the Law, the prophets, etc., and THIS was the period during which God's 'last' method of communication would be enjoyed, and under which the world would close. It might be a VERY LONG period, but it would be the 'last' one; and so far as the meaning of the phrase is concerned, it might be the longest period, or longer than all the others put together, but still it would be the 'last' one." *Barnes' Notes,* by Albert Barnes, D.D., (Electronic Database: Biblesoft, 1997), s.v. "Hebrews 1:2." All rights reserved.

Chapter 2

[1] "The Miracle Herd" by Lavitta Papan is reprinted by permission from *Acts Today: Signs and Wonders of the Holy Spirit,* by Ralph W. Harris (Springfield, Missouri: Gospel Publishing House, 1995), p. 65, 66.

Chapter 5

[1] JoAnne Gullickson, *On Angel's Wings,* (New York: Guidepost, 1998), p. 72.

Chapter 7

[1] Brown, Driver, Briggs and Gesenius, *The KJV Old Testament Hebrew Lexicon,* "Hebrew Lexicon entry for David," entry #1732, s.v. "David," available from <http://www.biblestudytools.net/Lexicons>.

Chapter 11

[1] Bob Davies and Lori Rentzel, *Coming Out of Homosexuality* (Downers Grove, Illinois: InterVarsity Press, January 1994).

Chapter 13

[1] Excerpts taken from *I Had No Father But God* by Paul Crouch, Sr. (Santa Ana, California: Trinity Broadcasting Network, 1993). Reprinted by permission.

Chapter 21

[1] Excerpts taken from *Nothing Is Impossible With God* by Kathryn Kuhlman (New York, New York: Pillar Books, 1974), s.v. "'So Much Left to Do,' SARA HOPKINS," pp. 221-231. Reprinted by permission.

[2] JoAnne Gullickson, *On Angel's Wings,* (New York: Guidepost, 1998), p. 76.

Chapter 27

[1] The Healing Rooms were started by John G. Lake over eighty years ago; they were reopened in July 1999, according to information from the Healing Rooms Web site, available from <http://www.healingrooms.com>.

Chapter 37

[1] "Promise Keepers is a Christ-centered organization dedicated to introducing men to Jesus Christ as their Savior and Lord; and then helping them to grow as Christians..." as stated on their Web site available from <http://www.promisekeepers.org>.

Chapter 53

[1] Margaret Mitchell, *Gone With the Wind,* (New York, New York: Scribner, 1996, reprint edition; originally published in 1936 by MacMillan). Rhett Butler is one of the main characters.

If you prayed the salvation prayer
to receive Jesus Christ as your
Lord and Savior for the first time,

Or you may write to us at

Harrison House

P.O. Box 35035

Tulsa, Oklahoma 74153

ABOUT THE AUTHORS

Sheri Stone

Sheri is Director of The International Network of Christians In The Arts, headquartered in Coeur d'Alene, Idaho. Sheri is coauthor of this anthology as well as a screenwriter with her husband, Gene, plus a student of music, art, journalism, and biblical expository. The Stones have been married for over 40 years.

Therese is a freelance writer, author of *Breaking Out* and co-author of this anthology. Her calling in the Body of Christ is to publish and teach hope and healing through Jesus Christ and His Word. Therese and her beloved husband, Tom, have three growing and active children.

Therese Marszalek

To contact Sheri Stone
or Therese Marszalek,
please write to:
Miracles Still Happen
P.O. Box 1754
Post Falls, Idaho 83877

Or by email at:
incnarts@earthlink.net
kingskids5@comcast.net

OTHER BOOKS BY SHERI STONE

Presently co-authoring
Plants of the Kingdom, Manna for Today
with Jini Craft

OTHER BOOKS BY
THERESE MARSZALEK

Breaking Out:
The Journey of Transformation
Into the Image of Jesus Christ

Additional copies of this book
are available at your local bookstore.

If this book has been a blessing to you
or if you would like to see more of
the Harrison House product line,

HARRISON HOUSE
Tulsa, Oklahoma 74153

THE HARRISON HOUSE VISION

Proclaiming the truth and the power
Of the Gospel of Jesus Christ
With excellence;

Challenging Christians to
Live victoriously,
Grow spiritually,
Know God intimately.